Mr. Boston Spirited Dessert Guide

MR. BOSTON SPIRITED DESSERT GUIDE

WARNER BOOKS

A Warner Communications Company

Recipes developed and tested under the supervision of the International Institute of Foods and Family Living, Inc., Chicago, Illinois.

Warner Books, Inc., 75 Rockefeller Plaza, New York, NY 10019

Printed in the United States of America

First printing: November 1982
10 9 8 7 6 5 4 3 2 1

Book design: H. Roberts Design

Library of Congress Cataloging in Publication Data

Mr. Boston spirited dessert guide.

Includes index.
1. Desserts. 2. Cookery (Liquors) I. Title:
Mister Boston spirited dessert guide.
TX773.M7 641.8′6 82-2638
ISBN 0-446-51253-2 AACR2

TABLE OF CONTENTS

Mr. Boston Spirited Dessert Guide

Introduction

From childhood, when they were a reward for eating vegetables, we have developed a special delight in desserts. They are often the high point of a meal, the beautiful denouement of an epicurean feast. What more appropriate than that desserts assume adult privilege—the right to adopt the accent of spirits, especially when liqueurs and liquors add so much character to each treat. And there's an added bonus—for the alcohol disappears in the baking, leaving the flavor with far fewer calories, the taste without the tipsy feeling.

There is, however, a technique to adding spirits to desserts, an expertise in combining flavors, in knowing how much is too much. That's where Mr. Boston becomes your guide. Following these recipes precisely you discover the point at which the addition of liquor does the most for a dessert, the liqueur that accentuates flavors most successfully. There is even a concluding chapter in the guide that shows you how to create your own do-it-yourself desserts in an unlimited variety.

But the recipes here are more than an initiation into preparing spirited desserts, they form a repertoire of magnificent dishes: from fruits to puddings, from soufflés to coffee cakes and breads, from cakes to pastries—all fit for your finest entertaining.

Fruit Desserts

There is more to the spirited fruit dessert than a quick dash of brandy added to a combination of apples, pears, and oranges. There are hot fruit desserts: fritters laced with liquor; desserts topped with liqueur-touched meringues. There are cold fruit desserts where the spirit is blended into cream. There are fruit extravaganzas in which two spirit flavors join in the sauce and brandy flambés the result. Whether you use fresh or frozen fruits, there is a cordial that can accent, contrast, or heighten the flavor, and turn a simple dessert into a special one.

APPLE FRITTERS

Blend rum and brandy; pour over apple slices and let stand at least 1 hour, turning slices several times. Drain and reserve marinade. Stir together dry ingredients. Beat together milk, egg, and reserved marinade; stir into dry ingredients until smooth. Dip apple slices in batter and deep-fat fry in hot oil until golden brown. Drain and sprinkle with confectioners' sugar. Serve warm.

8–10 servings

*Pears may also be used.

¼ cup Mr. Boston Virgin Islands Rum
2 tablespoons Mr. Boston Ginger Flavored Brandy
6 apples, cored, pared, and cut into ½-inch-thick round slices*
1 cup flour
2 tablespoons sugar
1½ teaspoons baking powder
½ teaspoon salt
¼ teaspoon nutmeg
½ cup milk
1 egg
Confectioners' sugar

MERINGUE-TOPPED APPLES SARONNO

Sprinkle apple slices with lemon juice. Combine 1 tablespoon sugar, 1 cup Amaretto di Saronno, 1 tablespoon orange peel, orange juice, and water in saucepan. Bring to a boil. Add apples and simmer 3–5 minutes or until apples are translucent but still firm. Remove apples and divide among six individual casseroles. Beat egg whites until foamy. Gradually add remaining 3 tablespoons sugar, 1 teaspoon Amaretto di Saronno, and 1 teaspoon orange peel and beat until stiff, but not dry, peaks form. Place meringue in pastry bag with a large star tip and pipe meringue decoratively over the apples. Bake in preheated 350° F. oven 15–20 minutes, or until lightly browned. Serve warm or cold.

6 servings

6 large cooking apples, peeled and sliced thick
¼ cup lemon juice
¼ cup sugar
1 cup plus 1 teaspoon Amaretto di Saronno
½ cup orange juice
½ cup water
1⅓ tablespoons grated orange peel
3 egg whites

MELON IN COGNAC

6 cups mixed melon balls or chunks
¾ cup Rémy Martin V.S.O.P. Cognac
⅔ cup honey
2 tablespoons lemon juice
2 cups sour cream

Blend melon, cognac, honey, and lemon juice. Cover and refrigerate 2–3 hours. Just before serving, stir in sour cream.

6–8 servings

GINGER STEWED APRICOTS

1 pound dried apricots
2 cups boiling water
⅓ cup Mr. Boston Ginger Flavored Brandy
½ cup sugar
½ cup honey

Cover apricots with boiling water; let stand 2 hours. Drain and reserve liquid. Combine reserved liquid, plus enough water to make 2 cups, with brandy, sugar, and honey. Bring to a boil, add apricots, reduce heat to low, and simmer 15 minutes. Remove from heat. Chill before serving.

4–6 servings

FLAMING STRAWBERRIES

- ¼ cup orange peel, in julienne strips
- ¼ cup sugar
- 2 tablespoons butter
- 2 tablespoons Mandarine Napoleon
- 2 tablespoons Mr. Boston Cherry Flavored Brandy
- 1 quart whole strawberries*
- 2 tablespoons Mr. Boston Five Star Brandy
- ½ cup orange juice

Cover orange peel with water, boil 5 minutes, and drain. Heat sugar over low heat until melted. Stir in butter and orange peel and cook, stirring constantly, 1 minute. Add Mandarine Napoleon and cherry brandy and bring to a boil. Reduce heat and stir in strawberries, heating just enough to coat with syrup. Pour brandy over berries and flambé. Stir in orange juice. Serve alone or over ice cream.

4–6 servings

*Well-drained pear halves may be substituted

STRAWBERRY SHERRY CREAM

- 6 cups strawberries, washed and hulled
- ½ cup confectioners' sugar
- ½ cup Balfour Cream Sherry
- 1 cup heavy cream, whipped

Reserve about 2 cups berries. Mash remaining berries with sugar and sherry. Fold in whipped cream. Gently fold whole berries into strawberry-cream mixture.

8–10 servings

WILD CHERRIES JUBILEE

- **2½ cups canned, pitted cherries and juice**
- **2 tablespoons cornstarch**
- **¼ cup Mr. Boston Cherry Flavored Brandy**
- **½ cup Mr. Boston Five Star Brandy**
- **1 quart vanilla ice cream**

Bring 1 cup cherry juice to boil in saucepan. Blend cornstarch and cherry brandy until smooth. Stir into hot liquid, stirring constantly, until smooth and thickened, 2–3 minutes. Add cherries and cook 2 minutes more. Pour remaining brandy over cherries and heat 1 minute. Ignite and, after flame dies, serve immediately over vanilla ice cream.

6 servings

EASY PEACH ALMOND COBBLER

- **½ cup butter or margarine, melted**
- **2 cups sliced peaches, fresh or thawed frozen**
- **½ cup plus 2 tablespoons sugar**
- **2 tablespoons Mr. Boston Crème de Noyaux**
- **1 cup flour**
- **½ tablespoon baking powder**
- **½ teaspoon salt**
- **¾ cup milk**

Pour melted butter into 8-inch square pan. Combine peaches, 2 tablespoons sugar, and Crème de Noyaux; let stand 10 minutes. Stir together ½ cup sugar and remaining dry ingredients; add milk and stir just until blended. Pour batter over melted butter, do not stir. Gently spoon peaches and syrup over batter. Bake in preheated 350°F. oven 45–55 minutes or until crust is golden brown. Serve warm or chilled.

6 servings

Merinque-Topped Apples Saronno

Melon in Cognac

ILLVA
AMARETTO
di
SARONNO
ORIGINALE

POACHED PEACHES

Combine Amaretto di Saronno, water, sugar, lemon, cinnamon, and nutmeg in saucepan. Bring to a boil. Add peach halves and re-heat to boiling. Reduce heat and simmer, covered, 12–15 minutes or until peaches are tender; remove peaches with slotted spoon. Continue cooking until liquid is reduced to 1½ cups, 15–20 minutes. Serve each peach with ¼ cup syrup.

6 servings

*Apples may also be used.

- **1 cup Amaretto di Saronno**
- **2 cups water**
- **3 tablespoons sugar**
- **½ lemon, sliced**
- **3 cinnamon sticks, halved**
- **½ teaspoon nutmeg**
- **6 peaches, peeled, halved, and pitted***

COUNTRY PEACH DESSERT

Place peaches flat side down in 7x11-inch baking pan. Drizzle with brandy and 1 tablespoon melted butter. Stir together flour, sugar, nutmeg, and salt. Stir in egg and remaining butter, blending until flour mixture is thoroughly moistened. Crumble over peaches. Bake in preheated 350°F. oven 25–30 minutes or until golden brown. Serve warm with cream.

6 servings

- **1 twenty-nine-ounce can peach halves, drained and halved**
- **3 tablespoons Mr. Boston Peach Flavored Brandy**
- **3 tablespoons butter, melted**
- **1 cup flour**
- **1 cup sugar**
- **¼ teaspoon nutmeg**
- **¼ teaspoon salt**
- **1 egg, beaten**

APRICOT STRAWBERRY TRIFLE

18 large ladyfingers
¾ cup apricot preserves
2 tablespoons Mr. Boston Apricot Flavored Brandy
Strawberry Cream (see below)
Whipped cream
Whole strawberries
Slivered almonds

Split ladyfingers, spread with apricot preserves, and reassemble. Spread more preserves on one side of whole ladyfingers and line 6-cup clear glass bowl or soufflé dish with ladyfingers, preserve side facing in. Sprinkle brandy over ladyfingers. Fill with strawberry cream and chill until firm, 3–4 hours. Garnish with whipped cream, whole berries, and slivered almonds.

6–8 servings

Strawberry Cream

2 eight-ounce packages cream cheese, softened
½ cup sugar
1 cup heavy cream
2 tablespoons Mr. Boston Apricot Flavored Brandy
3 cups sliced strawberries

Beat cream cheese and sugar until light and fluffy. Add cream and brandy and beat until light and thick. Fold in strawberries.

DIPLOMAT

Pour 3 tablespoons brandy over fruit and currants; let stand 30 minutes. Drain and reserve brandy. Sprinkle ladyfingers with remaining 5 tablespoons brandy. Line 6-cup mold with ladyfingers, keeping any extra for center. Beat together eggs, egg yolks, and sugar until light. Blend into hot milk and cook, stirring constantly, until slightly thickened. Stir in orange peel and reserved soaking brandy. Pour half the custard into prepared mold. Sprinkle with half the fruit mixture and half the preserves; cover with ladyfingers. Repeat with remaining custard, fruit, preserves, and ladyfingers. Place mold in pan of hot water and bake in preheated 325°F. oven 1 hour or until knife inserted near center comes out clean. Chill until firm. Unmold and top with Strawberry Sauce. Garnish with whole strawberries.

6–8 servings

½ cup Mr. Boston Five Star Brandy
⅔ cup mixed candied fruit
⅓ cup currants
40 ladyfingers
2 eggs
3 egg yolks
½ cup sugar
2 cups milk, scalded
1 tablespoon grated orange peel
⅓ cup apricot preserves, sieved
Strawberry Sauce (see below)
Whole strawberries

Strawberry Sauce

Purée strawberries with sugar and brandy. Strain.

3 cups sliced strawberries
3 tablespoons confectioner's sugar
2 tablespoons Mr. Boston Five Star Brandy

Soufflés and Puddings

Creamy, airy, custardy . . . boiled, baked, steamed or chilled . . . served hot or cold . . . with sauce or plain—soufflés and puddings make outstanding desserts. And they taste even better when the expansive personality of a cordial, liquor, or liqueur is added.

Whether you choose a hearty dessert such as Bread Pudding or a light, fluffy soufflé, you will have a grand finale.

SOUR CREAM SOUFFLÉ

Beat together egg yolks and sugar until thick and lemon-colored. Gradually blend in flour until smooth. Stir in sour cream and brandy. Beat egg whites until stiff, but not dry, peaks form. Fold egg whites into sour cream mixture. Pour into buttered 6-cup soufflé dish that has been fitted with a 2-inch foil collar and bake in preheated 350°F. oven 30–35 minutes or until center is firm. Serve immediately with warm Brandied Cherry Sauce.

6 servings

3 eggs, separated
½ cup sugar
½ cup flour
2 tablespoons Mr. Boston Cherry Flavored Brandy
1½ cups sour cream
Brandied Cherry Sauce (see below)

Brandied Cherry Sauce

Cut cherries in half and set aside. Bring reserved syrup to a boil. Blend water and cornstarch until smooth; blend into hot liquid, stirring constantly, until mixture is smooth and thickened. Cook 1 minute more. Remove from heat; stir in cherries and brandy.

1 sixteen-ounce can dark, sweet cherries, drained; reserve syrup
¼ cup cold water
2 tablespoons cornstarch
3 tablespoons Mr. Boston Cherry Flavored Brandy

GINGER APPLE SOUFFLÉ

- **5 eggs, separated**
- **1⅓ cups milk**
- **½ cup sugar**
- **⅓ cup flour**
- **½ teaspoon salt**
- **½ teaspoon cinnamon**
- **¼ teaspoon nutmeg**
- **⅛ teaspoon ground cloves**
- **1 cup shredded apple**
- **5 tablespoons Mr. Boston Ginger Flavored Brandy**

Combine egg yolks and milk. Stir together sugar, flour, salt, and spices. Blend liquid and dry ingredients until smooth and cook over medium heat, stirring constantly, until mixture thickens. Stir in apples and brandy and cook 4–5 minutes longer, stirring constantly. Set aside until slightly cooled. Beat egg whites until stiff, but not dry, peaks form. Fold cooled egg-yolk mixture into egg whites. Spoon mixture into buttered and sugared 1½-quart soufflé dish. Add aluminum foil collar if necessary. Bake in preheated 350°F. oven 40–45 minutes or until well browned. Serve immediately.

RASPBERRY SOUFFLÉ

- **2 tablespoons butter, melted**
- **3 tablespoons flour**
- **1 ten-ounce package frozen raspberries, well thawed and drained; reserve syrup**
- **½ cup sugar**
- **1 tablespoon lemon juice**
- **⅛ teaspoon salt**
- **4 egg yolks, well beaten**
- **¼ cup Mr. Boston Crème de Cassis**
- **5 egg whites**

Blend butter and flour until smooth. Add ½ cup reserved raspberry syrup, ¼ cup sugar, lemon juice, and salt. Cook, stirring constantly, over medium-low heat until mixture comes to a boil. Remove from heat. Beating constantly, add egg yolks in a thin stream. Return to heat and cook for 1 minute. Blend in crème de cassis and cool slightly. Beat egg whites until soft peaks form. Gradually add remaining ¼ cup sugar and beat until stiff, but not dry, peaks form. Fold yolk mixture into whites. Gently fold in well-drained raspberries. Pour into buttered and sugared 2-quart soufflé dish; bake on lower shelf in preheated 375°F. oven 30–35 minutes or until center is firm.

CHOCOLATE-COGNAC FLAN WITH CHOCOLATE SAUCE

Beat together eggs, sugar, cognac, crème de cacao, cocoa, and salt. Scald milk and beat into egg mixture. Pour into a buttered 8-inch round pan. Set pan in ½-inch hot water and bake in a preheated 350°F. oven 25–30 minutes or until done. Cool to room temperature. Run a knife around edge; turn out on serving plate; chill. Just before serving, spread warm Chocolate Sauce over flan. Cut into wedges.

8–10 servings

5 eggs
½ cup sugar
2 tablespoons Rémy Martin V.S.O.P. Cognac
2 tablespoons Mr. Boston Crème de Cacao
1 tablespoon cocoa
⅛ teaspoon salt
1⅓ cups milk
Chocolate Sauce (see below)

Chocolate Sauce

Melt chocolate chips in cream over low heat or in double boiler. Blend in crème de cacao until smooth. Serve over chilled flan.

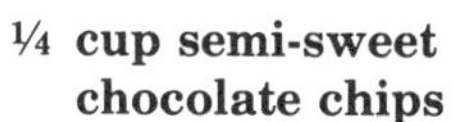

¼ cup semi-sweet chocolate chips
3 tablespoons heavy cream
1 tablespoon Mr. Boston Crème de Cacao

CREAMY ORANGE CARAMEL

¾ cup sugar
½ cup water
4 egg yolks
¼ cup Mr. Boston Triple Sec
2 cups half-and-half, scalded

Cook ½ cup sugar and water over medium heat, stirring frequently, until mixture turns a caramel color, about 10 minutes. Pour 1–2 tablespoons into each of 6 custard cups. Blend egg yolks, triple sec, and remaining ¼ cup sugar. Whisk hot half-and-half into egg-yolk mixture and beat until smooth. Pour equal amounts into custard cups. Set cups in 1 inch hot water in baking pan; bake in preheated 350°F. oven 55–60 minutes or until set. Unmold before serving. Serve at room temperature.

6 servings

FESTIVE KUGEL

1 cup light raisins
½ cup Rémy Martin V.S.O.P. Cognac
1 eight-ounce package cream cheese, softened
1 cup creamed cottage cheese
1½ cups milk
5 eggs, beaten
¾ cup sugar
1 teaspoon vanilla
½ teaspoon nutmeg
1 cup butter, softened
8 ounces dry fine noodles, cooked *al dente*
½ teaspoon cinnamon

Soak raisins in cognac 30 minutes. Beat cheeses until light and fluffy; blend in milk, eggs, sugar, vanilla, and nutmeg. Stir butter into cooked noodles. Blend noodles and raisin mixture into cheese mixture. Pour into buttered shallow 3-quart baking dish and sprinkle with cinnamon. Bake in preheated 350°F. oven 60–65 minutes or until set.

12 servings

LUSCIOUS LEMON MOUSSE

Sprinkle gelatin over 1/4 cup water and let stand 5 minutes. Heat water and gelatin, stirring constantly, until gelatin dissolves and mixture comes to a boil. Remove from heat and stir in lemon juice and peel. Chill 10–15 minutes. Beat together egg yolks, 1/2 cup sugar, and remaining 2 tablespoons water until thick and lemon-colored. Beat egg whites until foamy; gradually add remaining 1/2 cup sugar and beat until stiff, but not dry, peaks form. Fold cooled gelatin mixture into egg yolks. Fold egg-yolk mixture into egg whites. Beat cream until stiff. Add sherry and beat until stiff. Fold whipped cream into egg mixture. Pour into 6-cup soufflé dish with 2-inch collar attached. Chill 3–4 hours or until firm.

6–8 servings

- **1 envelope (1 tablespoon) unflavored gelatin**
- **6 tablespoons water**
- **1/2 cup lemon juice**
- **1 teaspoon grated lemon peel**
- **4 eggs, separated**
- **1 cup sugar**
- **1 cup heavy cream**
- **1/4 cup Balfour Cream Sherry**

MOCHA MOUSSE

Heat together milk and gelatin to boiling point, stirring to dissolve gelatin. Pour into blender with remaining ingredients except cream. Process until smooth. Fold blended mixture into whipped cream. Pour into a 1 1/2-quart mold. Chill until firm.

8 servings

- **1 1/2 cups milk**
- **1 envelope (1 tablespoon) unflavored gelatin**
- **1 cup semi-sweet chocolate chips**
- **1/4 cup Mr. Boston Crème de Cacao**
- **1/4 cup Expresso Coffee Liqueur**
- **1 egg**
- **1/4 cup sugar**
- **1/8 teaspoon salt**
- **1 cup heavy cream, whipped**

PUMPKIN MOLD WITH GINGER CREAM SAUCE

- 2 envelopes (2 tablespoons) unflavored gelatin
- 6 tablespoons water
- 1 16-ounce can pumpkin
- 1 cup brown sugar, packed
- ¼ cup Amaretto di Saronno
- ½ teaspoon cinnamon
- ¼ teaspoon vanilla
- ⅛ teaspoon salt
- 2 cups heavy cream, whipped
- Ginger Cream Sauce (see below)

Sprinkle gelatin over water in saucepan and let stand 5 minutes. Heat and stir until gelatin dissolves and mixture comes to boil. Remove from heat. Combine gelatin with pumpkin, brown sugar, Amaretto di Saronno, cinnamon, vanilla, and salt; stir to blend well. Fold whipped cream into pumpkin mixture. Pour into oiled 6-cup mold. Refrigerate overnight. Unmold and serve with Ginger Cream Sauce.

8–10 servings

Ginger Cream Sauce

- 2 tablespoons finely chopped, candied ginger
- 2 tablespoons butter
- ½ cup heavy cream

Melt ginger in butter and cream. Cook over low heat, stirring constantly, until mixture thickens. Remove from heat and chill. Serve over Pumpkin Mold.

FLOATING ISLAND SARONNO

6 egg whites
½ cup sugar
¼ cup Amaretto di Saronno
Vanilla Sauce (see below)

Beat egg whites until foamy; gradually add ¼ cup sugar and beat until soft peaks form. Add remaining sugar and beat until stiff, but not dry, peaks form. Fold in Amaretto di Saronno and spoon into buttered and sugared 10-inch ring mold. Place buttered aluminum foil on top to prevent browning. Set ring mold in 2 inches of hot water in pan and bake in preheated 350°F. oven 30 minutes. Cool and unmold into Vanilla Sauce. Cut into wedges and serve with sauce.

8 servings

Vanilla Sauce

2 cups milk, scalded
1 teaspoon vanilla
4 egg yolks
½ cup sugar

Blend hot milk and vanilla. Beat together egg yolks and sugar until smooth. Gradually blend milk mixture into egg-yolk mixture in saucepan. Cook over low heat, stirring constantly, until mixture thickens slightly, 10–15 minutes. Remove from heat, cool to room temperature, and chill. Pour chilled sauce into deep 12-inch platter.

TRADITIONAL BREAD PUDDING WITH BRANDY SAUCE

- **12 slices day-old white bread, crusts trimmed, and cut in half diagonally**
- **4 cups milk**
- **4 eggs**
- **1 cup sugar**
- **½ teaspoon salt**
- **1 tablespoon butter**
- **Nutmeg**
- **Peach Brandy Sauce (see below)**

Place a single layer of bread in buttered 2-quart shallow baking dish. Arrange remaining bread on top in two rows, overlapping slices. Beat together milk, eggs, sugar, and salt. Pour over bread and let stand 10–15 minutes. Press bread as it softens to fully immerse it in liquid. Dot with butter and sprinkle with nutmeg. Bake in preheated 350°F. oven 45 minutes or until set. Serve chilled with warm Peach Brandy Sauce.

8 servings

Peach Brandy Sauce

- **½ cup cold water**
- **1 tablespoon cornstarch**
- **½ cup Mr. Boston Peach Flavored Brandy**
- **¼ cup sugar**
- **2 tablespoons peach preserves**
- **2 tablespoons butter**

Blend water and cornstarch in saucepan until smooth. Stir in remaining ingredients. Bring to a boil, stirring occasionally. Reduce heat and simmer 5 minutes. Serve warm.

INDIAN PUDDING

- **2 eggs, beaten**
- **5 cups milk**
- **1 cup Mr. Boston Virgin Islands Light Rum**
- **½ cup molasses**
- **¼ cup sugar**
- **¼ teaspoon baking soda**
- **¼ teaspoon salt**
- **1 cup corn meal**
- **¼ cup butter**

Blend together eggs, 3 cups milk, rum, molasses, sugar, soda, and salt in saucepan. Cook over medium heat, stirring constantly, until molasses and sugar dissolve and mixture comes to a boil. Reduce heat, gradually add corn meal, stirring constantly, until corn meal is completely blended. Cook, uncovered, stirring occasionally, until mixture is thickened. Remove from heat and beat in butter and remaining 2 cups milk. Pour into buttered 2-quart baking dish and bake in preheated 350°F. oven 1 hour. Reduce heat to 300°F. and bake 1 hour more or until pudding is firm. Serve warm with whipped cream or vanilla ice cream.

6 servings

BLACK-BOTTOM PUDDING PIE

For the crust:

1½ cups flour
1 teaspoon salt
½ cup shortening
3–6 tablespoons cold water

Stir together flour and salt. Cut in shortening until mixture resembles coarse crumbs. Sprinkle with water, 1–2 tablespoons at a time, mixing lightly until dough forms a ball. Roll out on lightly floured surface to 11-inch circle and loosely fit into 9-inch pie pan. Trim pastry and flute edges. Prick inside with fork. Bake in preheated 400°F. oven 10–12 minutes or until golden brown.

For the filling:

2 one-ounce squares unsweetened chocolate
1½ cups heavy cream
¾ cup sugar
2 eggs, separated
¼ cup Mr. Boston Coffee Flavored Brandy
½ cup chopped hazelnuts or pecans
1 envelope unflavored gelatin
3 tablespoons water

Heat chocolate and ¼ cup cream over hot water until chocolate melts. Add ¼ cup sugar, 1 egg yolk, and 1 tablespoon brandy, and cook, stirring constantly, until slightly thickened. Remove from heat, stir in nuts, and pour over bottom of baked pie crust. Chill until firm. Sprinkle gelatin over water and let stand 5 minutes. Cook gelatin over low heat until dissolved. Blend in remaining ½ cup sugar, 1 egg yolk, and ½ cup cream. Cook over low heat, stirring constantly, until mixture thickens slightly. Remove from heat and stir in remaining 3 tablespoons brandy. Chill until mixture just begins to gel, about 20 minutes. Beat egg whites until stiff, but not dry, peaks form. Beat remaining ¾ cup cream until stiff. Fold egg whites, then whipped cream, into brandy mixture. Spoon into pie shell and chill until firm, 3–4 hours. Garnish with chocolate curls and chopped nuts.

one 9-inch pie

Flaming Strawberries

Mocha Mousse

STRAWBERRY RICE CREAM

Combine strawberries and brandy and let stand 30–40 minutes. Cover rice with boiling water and let stand 30 minutes; drain well. Combine rice with 2 cups milk and salt. Cook, covered, 25 minutes or until rice is tender. Sprinkle gelatin over water and let stand 5 minutes. Combine sugar and egg yolks; mix well. Stir in remaining 1 cup milk and cook, stirring constantly, over low heat until slightly thickened. Add gelatin and cook, stirring constantly until gelatin is dissolved. Strain custard mixture into rice; mix well. Chill until mixture begins to set, about 30 minutes. Fold strawberries, whipped cream, and vanilla into chilled mixture. Pour into lightly oiled 1-quart mold. Chill until set, 5–6 hours. Unmold and decorate with strawberries and whipped cream.

6–8 servings

1½ cups sliced strawberries
¼ cup Mr. Boston Five Star Brandy
½ cup long grain rice
1 cup boiling water
3 cups milk
¼ teaspoon salt
2 teaspoons unflavored gelatin
2 tablespoons water
¼ cup sugar
2 large egg yolks
½ cup heavy cream, whipped
1½ teaspoons vanilla extract
Whole strawberries
Whipped cream

MOCHA FONDUE

Melt chocolate over hot water. Blend in cream and brandy until smooth. Hold over hot water until ready to serve. Serve in ceramic fondue pot or dish with fruit.

4–6 servings

1 six-ounce package semi-sweet chocolate chips
½ cup heavy cream
¼ cup Mr. Boston Coffee Flavored Brandy
4 cups fresh fruit in bite-size pieces

Frozen Desserts

The perfect dessert from the standpoint of the cook is one that can be prepared in advance, appear at the table cooly elegant, and surprise the palates of the guests with its subtle, unique flavor. The desserts that follow satisfy all those requirements. Whether you choose the simple Mandarine Cream or the elaborate Ice Cream Bombe with Blackberry Brandy Sauce; whether you use an ice cream freezer or an ice cube tray in your refrigerator; whether you start with basic ingredients such as eggs, milk, and sugar or begin with a bakery pound cake or a good commercial ice cream—you can produce a dessert worthy of any epicure. Rely on the recipes in this section for desserts that are everything you would hope for—cold, captivating, and complemented by the judicious addition of spirits.

MANDARINE CREAM

Beat Mandarine Napoleon into ice cream. Serve immediately.

4 servings

- **⅓ cup Mandarine Napoleon**
- **1 pint vanilla, chocolate, or strawberry ice cream, slightly softened**

COUPES NAPOLEON

Halve oranges and remove fruit in sections. Clean out inside of shells and refrigerate. Marinate orange sections in Mandarine Napoleon about 2 hours. Stir 3 tablespoons marinade into sherbet, mixing well. Spoon sherbet mixture into shells and freeze until firm. Top with orange sections before serving.

4 servings

- **2 seedless oranges**
- **3 tablespoons Mandarine Napoleon**
- **1 pint lemon sherbet, slightly softened**

FROSTY GINGER SOUFFLÉ

- **4 eggs, separated**
- **⅔ cup sugar**
- **½ cup Mr. Boston Ginger Flavored Brandy**
- **2 tablespoons lime juice**
- **1 teaspoon grated lime peel**
- **1 tablespoon finely chopped, candied ginger**
- **2 cups heavy cream, whipped**

Beat together egg yolks and sugar until thick and lemon-colored. Stir in brandy, lime juice and peel, and ginger. Beat egg whites until stiff, but not dry, peaks form. Fold first the egg whites, then the whipped cream into brandy mixture. Pour into 1½-quart soufflé dish. Add aluminum foil collar if necessary. Freeze until firm, about 3 hours. Remove collar before serving.

8–10 servings

SOUFFLÉ GLACÉ À L'ORANGE

- **6 eggs, separated**
- **¾ cup plus 2 tablespoons sugar**
- **½ cup lemon juice**
- **½ cup orange juice**
- **½ teaspoon grated lemon peel**
- **½ teaspoon grated orange peel**
- **3 tablespoons Mr. Boston Triple Sec**
- **2 tablespoons Mandarine Napoleon**
- **Chocolate, semi-sweet (optional)**

Combine egg yolks, ½ cup sugar, fruit juices and peels, and liqueurs in top of double boiler. Cook over simmering, not boiling, water until mixture thickens, 10–15 minutes. Remove from heat and cool* to room temperature. Beat egg whites until foamy; gradually add remaining 6 tablespoons sugar and beat until stiff, but not dry, peaks form. Fold cooled custard into meringue. Pour into 2-quart soufflé dish. Cover and freeze at least 4 hours. Just before serving, garnish with shaved chocolate, if desired.

6–8 servings

*Custard may be cooled more rapidly by placing top of double boiler in bowl of ice water.

FROZEN BANANA VELVET MOUSSE

Place bananas and ¼ cup cream in blender jar or food processor and blend until smooth. Combine bananas, pineapple, and Mandarine Napoleon. Beat remaining ¾ cup cream until stiff; beat in sugar and brandy. Fold into banana mixture. Pour into individual serving dishes, cover, and freeze. Let stand at room temperature 15 minutes before serving. Garnish with whipped cream, if desired.

6–8 servings

6 ripe bananas, cut in chunks
1 cup heavy cream
1 sixteen-ounce can crushed pineapple, drained
⅓ cup Mandarine Napoleon
2 tablespoons confectioners' sugar
1 teaspoon Mr. Boston Five Star Brandy
Whipped cream (optional)

ICE CREAM BOMBE WITH BLACKBERRY BRANDY SAUCE

½ gallon vanilla ice cream
2 cups finely chopped peaches
3 tablespoons Mr. Boston Peach Flavored Brandy
1 pint raspberry sherbet
Whipped cream
Blackberry Brandy Sauce (see below)

Combine 1 quart ice cream, peaches, and brandy and pack firmly and equally against bottom and sides of chilled 2½-quart bowl or mold. Freeze 2–2½ hours or until firm. Make second layer with remaining 1 quart ice cream. Freeze until firm. Combine sherbet and ¼ cup Blackberry Brandy Sauce; place in center of bowl or mold. Cover and freeze overnight. Unmold on serving platter and freeze until ready to serve. Just before serving garnish with whipped cream rosettes. Serve wedges with Blackberry Brandy Sauce.

10–12 servings

Blackberry Brandy Sauce

1 twelve-ounce jar seedless blackberry or black raspberry jam
⅔ cup water
3 cups fresh blackberries or 1 sixteen-ounce package frozen unsweetened blackberries
2 half-inch strips lemon peel
¼ cup Mr. Boston Blackberry Flavored Brandy
2 tablespoons cornstarch

Combine jam and water in saucepan; cook over medium heat, stirring constantly, until smooth. Bring to a boil and add blackberries and lemon peel. Return to boil, reduce heat, and simmer until blackberries are tender, about 5 minutes. Blend brandy and cornstarch, stir into blackberry mixture, and cook, stirring constantly, until thickened.

CHOCOLATE ALMOND ICE CREAM

Combine eggs, milk, sugar, chocolate, and salt. Cook over medium-low heat, stirring constantly, until chocolate melts and mixture thickens slightly, 10–15 minutes. Remove from heat, stir in Amaretto di Saronno, and chill. Whip cream and fold into chocolate mixture. Place mixture in ice-cream freezer packed with 4 parts crushed ice to 1 part rock salt. Churn until stiff. Serve immediately or store in freezer until ready to serve.

4–6 servings

3 eggs, beaten
1 cup milk
½ cup sugar
2 squares (2 ounces) unsweetened chocolate
⅛ teaspoon salt
¼ cup Amaretto di Saronno
1 cup heavy cream, partially frozen
½ cup chopped almonds

STRAWBERRY ICE CREAM ROLL

Beat egg yolks until thick and lemon-colored; gradually beat in ½ cup sugar until very thick and creamy. Stir in 1 tablespoon cognac. Beat egg whites until foamy; gradually add remaining ¼ cup sugar and beat until stiff, but not dry, peaks form. Fold egg yolks into egg-white mixture. Sprinkle flour over egg mixture and gently fold until well blended. Pour into 15½x10½-inch jelly-roll pan lined with greased wax paper. Bake in preheated 375°F. oven 12–15 minutes or until lightly browned. Turn immediately onto clean towel that has been heavily dusted with confectioners' sugar. Remove wax paper. Beginning at narrow end, roll up cake and towel, jelly-roll fashion. Cool cake completely. Combine ice cream, strawberries, and remaining cognac. Unroll cake, spread with ice cream, and re-roll without towel. Freeze until firm, about 2 hours. Slice and serve.

10–12 servings

4 eggs, separated
¾ cup sugar
3 tablespoons Rémy Martin V.S.O.P. Cognac
¾ cup flour
Confectioners' sugar
1 quart vanilla ice cream, softened
1 cup sliced strawberries

PEPPERMINT SCHNAPPS PARFAITS

- 1 six-ounce package semi-sweet chocolate chips
- ½ cup heavy cream
- 3–4 tablespoons Mr. Boston Peppermint Schnapps
- 1 pint strawberry ice cream
- 1 pint pistachio ice cream
- 1 pint vanilla ice cream
- Whipped cream
- Maraschino cherries
- Chopped nuts

Cook chocolate, cream, and sugar over low heat, stirring constantly, until sugar is dissolved and chocolate is melted, about 5 minutes. Stir in peppermint schnapps and blend until smooth. Remove sauce from heat and allow to cool. Layer sauce with ice creams in six stemmed parfait glasses, reserving a little sauce to drizzle over top. Garnish with whipped cream, cherries, and nuts. Drizzle with reserved sauce. Freeze until ready to serve.

6 servings

PEAR SORBET

- 1¼ cups pear purée
- ½ cup Mr. Boston Triple Sec
- ½ cup orange juice
- 2 tablespoons sugar
- 2 tablespoons lemon juice

Combine pear purée, triple sec, orange juice, sugar, and lemon juice. Pour into a 1-quart freezer tray and freeze until mushy, stirring occasionally. Beat until smooth. Return to tray and freeze until firm, stirring once or twice.

4–5 servings

SNOWBALL

Stir together candied fruit and 2 tablespoons anisette; let stand 1 hour. Beat egg yolks and sugar until thick and lemon-colored. Blend in flour, lime juice, and peel. Beat egg whites until stiff, but not dry, peaks form; fold into flour-yolk mixture. Pour batter into two greased and floured 1-quart ovenproof bowls. Bake in preheated 325°F. oven 40–45 minutes or until cake springs back when lightly pressed. Cool slightly, remove from bowls, and cool completely. Cut horizontal slice from each cake so that when cakes are put together they form a sphere; reserve slices. Carve out inside of cake, leaving 1-inch shell. Sprinkle shell with brandy. Blend candied fruit with ice cream and place half in each cake shell. Freeze until firm. Blend whipped cream, confectioners' sugar, and remaining 1 tablespoon anisette. Use reserved slices for base. Spread whipped cream mixture between and over top of slices. Form ball with ice cream-filled cake halves; set on base. Frost with remaining whipped cream. Freeze until ready to serve.

8–10 servings

- **½ cup finely chopped candied fruit**
- **3 tablespoons Mr. Boston Anisette**
- **5 eggs, separated**
- **½ cup sugar**
- **¾ cup sifted flour**
- **1 tablespoon lime juice**
- **1 teaspoon grated lime peel**
- **2 tablespoons Mr. Boston Five Star Brandy**
- **1 pint vanilla or chocolate ice cream, softened**
- **1½ cups heavy cream, whipped**
- **2 tablespoons confectioners' sugar**

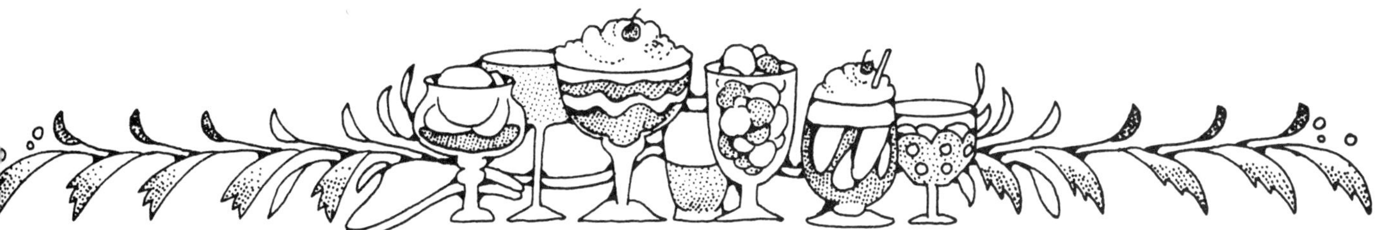

COFFEE ICE

3½ cups strong, hot coffee
1½ cups Mr. Boston Coffee Flavored Brandy
⅓ cup light brown sugar, packed
Sweetened whipped cream

Combine coffee, brandy, and sugar; stir until sugar is dissolved. Place in freezer and let stand until almost firm, 5–6 hours. Remove from freezer and beat until smooth. Return to freezer and freeze until firm, but slightly mushy. Serve in glasses topped with whipped cream.

8–10 servings

RASPBERRY CURRANT SORBET

¾ cup red currant jelly
2 ten-ounce packages frozen raspberries, thawed and drained; reserve ½ cup syrup
⅓ cup Mr. Boston Virgin Islands Light Rum

Combine jelly, reserved raspberry syrup, and rum. Bring to a boil, stirring constantly, until jelly is dissolved. Cool mixture and stir in raspberries. Place in ice-cream freezer. Surround with 4 parts crushed ice to 1 part rock salt and churn until stiff. Remove dasher and repack in ice and salt. Let stand 1 hour before serving.

4–6 servings

BLUEBERRY SHERBET

Combine blueberries and sherry in saucepan; cook, covered, over medium heat until blueberries are tender, 6–8 minutes. Cool and purée. Stir in remaining ingredients and place in ice-cream freezer. Surround with 4 parts crushed ice to 1 part rock salt and churn until stiff. Remove dasher, repack in ice and salt, and let stand 1 hour before serving.

8–10 servings

4 cups blueberries
½ cup Balfour Cream Sherry
½ cup sugar
2 tablespoons lemon juice
1¾ cups light cream
½ teaspoon grated lemon peel

CRÈME DE MENTHE SHERBET

Combine sugar and water in saucepan; boil until sugar dissolves. Remove from heat. Stir in crème de menthe and lemon juice. Freeze in pan or freezer tray until mushy, 2–2½ hours. Beat egg whites until stiff, but not dry, peaks form. Remove mint mixture from freezer and beat until smooth. Fold in beaten egg whites, blending until smooth. Return mixture to freezer tray and freeze until firm.

8 servings

¾ cup sugar
1 cup water
¼ cup Mr. Boston Crème de Menthe (green)
¼ cup lemon juice
Few drops green food coloring
2 egg whites

BLACK RASPBERRY CAKE ROLL

4 eggs, separated
¾ cup sugar
1 tablespoon grated orange peel
½ teaspoon ground ginger
1 cup flour
½ teaspoon baking powder
¼ teaspoon salt
Confectioners' sugar
1 quart raspberry sherbet, softened
5 tablespoons Mr. Boston Blackberry Flavored Brandy
2 cups sweetened blackberries

Beat egg yolks and ¼ cup sugar until thick and lemon-colored. Stir in orange peel and ginger. Beat egg whites until foamy; gradually add remaining ½ cup sugar and beat until stiff, but not dry, peaks form. Fold egg-yolk mixture into egg whites. Stir together flour, baking powder, and salt; sprinkle over eggs and gently fold into mixture until well blended. Pour into wax paper-lined 15½x10½-inch jelly-roll pan. Bake in preheated 375°F. oven 12–15 minutes or until very lightly browned. Immediately turn onto a clean towel that has been heavily dusted with confectioners' sugar. Remove wax paper. Beginning at narrow end, roll up cake and towel, jelly-roll fashion. Cool completely. Blend softened sherbet with 3 tablespoons brandy. Unroll cake; spread with sherbet mixture and re-roll cake without towel. Place in freezer for about 2 hours or until firm. Stir remaining 2 tablespoons brandy into blackberries. Serve blackberries over slices of cake roll.

10–12 servings

STRAWBERRY MOCHA CASSATA

Line 9x5-inch loaf pan with cheesecloth. Cut frozen pound cake lengthwise into six slices. Trim crust. Line bottom and sides of pan with cake, trimming to fit. Brush cake with 2 tablespoons crème de cacao. Combine ¾ cup sugar, cocoa, coffee, Amaretto di Saronno, and cook over medium heat, stirring constantly, until sugar dissolves and mixture boils. Remove from heat; cool to room temperature. Beat egg yolks until light and fluffy. Gradually add chocolate mixture and continue beating until thickened, about 5 minutes. Chill 20–30 minutes. Beat 1 cup cream until stiff; fold into chocolate mixture. Spread chocolate mixture equally over bottom and sides of cake-lined loaf pan, leaving center open. Cover and freeze until partially firm, 1½–2 hours. Combine strawberries and remaining 4 tablespoons crème de cacao; let stand 30 minutes. Beat egg whites until stiff, but not dry, peaks form. Beat remaining 1 cup cream until stiff. Fold strawberries and whipped cream into egg whites and blend thoroughly. Re-spread chocolate mixture over sides, if necessary. Spoon strawberry mixture into center. Cover and freeze until firm, 5–6 hours or overnight. Unmold and spread Chocolate Glaze over top and sides. Freeze until ready to serve.

8–10 servings

- **10¾ ounces frozen pound cake**
- **6 tablespoons Mr. Boston Crème de Cacao (white)**
- **1 cup sugar**
- **2 tablespoons cocoa**
- **1 tablespoon instant coffee**
- **¼ cup Amaretto di Saronno**
- **4 eggs, separated**
- **2 cups heavy cream**
- **1½ cups chopped strawberries**
- **Chocolate Glaze (see below)**

Chocolate Glaze

Cook all ingredients over medium heat, stirring constantly, 10–12 minutes or until thickened slightly. Cool to room temperature.

- **¾ cup cocoa**
- **½ cup sugar**
- **½ cup milk**
- **¼ cup Amaretto di Saronno**
- **⅓ cup butter**

Floating Island Saronno & Traditional Bread Pudding with Brandy Sauce

Coupes Napoleon

Cakes

Whether they are added to the frosting, the filling, the layers, the crumbs, or the total product, spirits in any cake make their presence known distinctively and deliciously. The herbs, flavorings, and aromatics of spirits make superb what before was merely good. The difference may be subtle yet irresistible, or bold and decisive—but it will always be superior.

So make your cake old-fashioned, hearty, and unadorned by icing. Or build it in careful, textured tiers. In either case, follow the recipe precisely, since the relation in cake of one ingredient to another is critical.

CHOCOLATE MOUSSE CAKE SARONNO

- **1 cup semi-sweet chocolate chips, melted**
- **18 whole blanched almonds**
- **½ cup Amaretto di Saronno**
- **2 envelopes (2 tablespoons) unflavored gelatin**
- **¼ cup water**
- **4 eggs, separated**
- **⅓ cup sugar**
- **2 cups milk**
- **2 cups heavy cream, whipped**
- **2 three-ounce packages lady fingers, split**

Dip bottom half of each almond in melted chocolate; chill until firm. Stir Amaretto di Saronno into remaining chocolate; set aside. Combine gelatin, water, egg yolks, sugar, and milk in saucepan. Cook, stirring constantly, over low heat until mixture thickens slightly. Stir in chocolate; chill until mixture mounds. Beat egg whites until stiff and fold into chocolate mixture. Fold 1 cup whipped cream into chocolate mixture, reserving remaining 1 cup. Line bottom and sides of 9-inch springform pan with split lady fingers and cover evenly with chocolate mixture. Chill until firm, 3–4 hours. Remove sides of pan and pipe whipped cream rosettes around top and bottom edges of cake. Press 1 almond chocolate end out into each rosette. Chill until ready to serve.

one 9-inch cake

MOCHA CHEESECAKE SARONNO

- **1 cup flour**
- **¼ cup sugar**
- **1 tablespoon grated lemon peel**
- **½ cup butter or margarine**
- **1 egg yolk**
- **4 eight-ounce packages cream cheese, softened**
- **1½ cups sugar**
- **¼ teaspoon salt**
- **5 eggs**
- **⅓ cup Amaretto di Saronno**
- **2 tablespoons instant coffee**
- **Sweetened whipped cream**

Stir together flour, sugar, and lemon peel. Cut in butter until mixture resembles coarse crumbs. Add egg yolk and mix until dough forms ball. Cover and chill 1 hour. Pat dough evenly over bottom and sides of an ungreased 10-inch springform pan. Beat cream cheese until fluffy. Beat in sugar and salt. Beat in eggs, one at a time, beating well after each addition. Blend Amaretto di Saronno and coffee until coffee is dissolved; beat into cheese mixture. Pour into dough-lined pan. Bake in a preheated 250°F. oven 1½–2 hours or until center is firm. Cool cake and chill. Remove sides of pan and decorate top of cake with rosettes of sweetened whipped cream. Dust rosettes with instant coffee.

one 10-inch cheesecake

BROWN SUGAR BEER CAKE

- ½ cup butter, softened
- 1 cup light brown sugar, packed
- 4 eggs, separated
- 3 cups flour
- 1½ tablespoons baking powder
- 1½ teaspoons salt
- 1½ cups stale beer
- Butter Glaze (see below)

Beat together butter and sugar until light and fluffy. Add egg yolks and beat well. Stir together flour, baking powder, and salt. Blend flour mixture alternately with beer into creamed mixture, beginning and ending with flour. Beat egg whites until stiff, but not dry, peaks form; gently fold into batter. Pour batter into greased and floured 10-inch tube pan. Bake in preheated 350°F. oven for about 1 hour or until golden brown. Cool 10 minutes before removing from pan. Frost with Butter Glaze.

one 10-inch cake

Butter Glaze

- ¼ cup butter
- 1 cup confectioners' sugar
- 1 teaspoon vanilla
- 1–2 tablespoons hot water

Heat butter until golden brown. Remove from heat. Beat in sugar and vanilla. Add enough water to make a glaze. Spread on cooled cake.

PUMPKIN CAKE

4 eggs
1 cup sugar
1 cup light brown sugar, packed
1 sixteen-ounce can pumpkin
1 cup vegetable oil
2 tablespoons Mr. Boston Virgin Islands Dark Rum
3 cups flour
2 teaspoons pumpkin pie spice
1½ tablespoons baking powder
1½ teaspoons salt
Chocolate Glaze (see below)

Beat eggs until frothy; add sugars and beat until very thick. Add pumpkin, oil, and rum; blend until smooth. Stir together flour, spice, baking powder, and salt. Thoroughly blend flour mixture into creamed mixture. Pour into greased and floured 10-inch tube or bundt cake pan. Bake in preheated 350°F. oven about 1 hour or until cake tester inserted near center comes out clean. Cool 10 minutes before removing from pan. Cool completely on wire rack. Drizzle with Chocolate Glaze.

one 10-inch cake

Chocolate Glaze

1 tablespoon butter
1 square (1 ounce) unsweetened chocolate
2 tablespoons Mr. Boston Virgin Islands Dark Rum
1¼ cups confectioners' sugar
2–3 tablespoons milk

Melt butter and chocolate in saucepan. Stir in rum. Add sugar alternately with milk until drizzling consistency is reached.

YOGURT CAKE

- 1 cup butter, softened
- 1½ cups sugar
- 6 eggs, separated
- 2½ cups flour
- 1 teaspoon baking soda
- ¼ teaspoon salt
- 1 cup boysenberry yogurt
- ¼ cup Mr. Boston Crème de Cassis

Beat together butter and 1¼ cups of the sugar until light and fluffy. Add egg yolks and beat until mixture is thick and lemon-colored. Stir together flour, soda, and salt. Blend yogurt and crème de cassis. Blend flour mixture alternately with yogurt mixture into creamed mixture, beginning and ending with flour mixture. Beat egg whites until soft peaks form; gradually add remaining ¼ cup sugar, beating until stiff, but not dry, peaks form. Fold batter into beaten egg whites and pour into a greased 10-inch bundt or tube pan. Bake in preheated 350°F. oven 45–50 minutes or until done. Cool in pan 15 minutes before removing.

12 servings

DUNDEE CAKE

- ½ cup currants
- ½ cup golden raisins
- ¼ cup Mandarine Napoleon
- ½ cup butter, softened
- ½ cup sugar
- ⅔ cup orange marmalade
- 1 teaspoon vanilla
- 2 eggs
- 2½ cups flour
- 1 tablespoon baking powder
- 1 teaspoon salt
- ¾ teaspoon allspice
- ¾ cup milk
- ¼ cup sliced almonds

Combine currants, raisins, and Mandarine Napoleon; let stand 1 hour. Beat together butter and sugar until light and fluffy. Add marmalade and beat until smooth and fluffy. Add vanilla and eggs, one at a time, beating well after each addition. Stir together flour, baking powder, salt, and allspice. Add flour mixture alternately with milk to creamed mixture, beginning and ending with flour. Stir in the currants and raisins and all but 1 tablespoon of the almonds. Pour batter into well-greased 9x5-inch loaf pan. Sprinkle top with remaining almonds. Bake in preheated 350°F. oven 55–65 minutes or until wooden pick inserted near center comes out clean. Cool in pan 10 minutes. Remove from pan and cool completely on wire rack before serving.

one 9x5-inch cake

BOLO DE LARANGA

½ cup butter
1¼ cups sugar
1 teaspoon grated orange peel
3 eggs, separated
¾ cup orange juice
¼ cup Mr. Boston Triple Sec
½ cup milk
2 cups flour
1 tablespoon baking powder
1 teaspoon salt
½ teaspoon baking soda
Whipped cream (optional)

Beat together butter and 1 cup sugar until light and fluffy. Add orange peel and egg yolks, one at a time, beating well after each addition. Blend orange juice and triple sec. Combine ½ cup orange juice mixture with milk. Stir together flour, baking powder, salt, and baking soda. Add flour mixture and milk mixture alternately to creamed mixture, beginning and ending with flour. Beat egg whites until stiff, but not dry, peaks form; gently fold into batter. Pour into greased and floured 9-inch square baking pan. Bake in preheated 350° F. oven 35–40 minutes. Cake will be very dark brown on top. Combine remaining ½ cup orange juice mixture and remaining ¼ cup sugar. Pour mixture over hot cake. Cool before serving. Top with whipped cream, if desired.

one 9-inch square cake

BANANA SURPRISE CAKE

Beat together sugar and shortening until light and fluffy. Add eggs, one at a time, beating well after each addition. Stir together flour, baking powder, and salt. Combine mashed banana, milk, and crème de banana. Add flour mixture to creamed mixture alternately with banana mixture, beginning and ending with flour. Add cooled melted chocolate and crème de cacao to 1 cup of the batter; blend thoroughly. Pour remaining batter into generously greased and floured 6-cup fluted mold. Spoon chocolate batter in a ring in center of light batter; press it gently into light batter. Bake in preheated 350°F. oven 50–60 minutes or until tester inserted near center comes out clean. Cool 10 minutes in pan. Remove and cool completely. Dust with confectioners' sugar.

one 8-inch round cake

1¼ cups sugar
½ cup shortening
2 eggs
2 cups flour
1 tablespoon baking powder
1 teaspoon salt
⅓ mashed ripe banana
¼ cup milk
3 tablespoons Mr. Boston Crème de Banana
1 square (1 ounce) unsweetened chocolate, melted
1 tablespoon Mr. Boston Crème de Cacao
Confectioners' sugar

SOUR MASH POUND CAKE

Beat together butter and sugar until light and fluffy. Add eggs, one at a time, beating well after each addition. Stir together flour, nutmeg, and candied fruit. Blend into creamed mixture alternately with bourbon. Pour into greased and floured 9- or 10-inch bundt cake pan. Bake in preheated 325°F. oven 60–70 minutes or until cake tester inserted near center comes out clean. Remove from pan. Cool. Dust with confectioners' sugar.

one 9- or 10-inch cake

1 cup butter, softened
1⅔ cups sugar
5 eggs
2 cups flour
¼ teaspoon nutmeg
½ cup finely chopped, mixed candied fruit
¼ cup Yellowstone Mellow Mash
Confectioners' sugar

COFFEE WALNUT ROLL

4 eggs, separated
⅓ cup sugar
1 tablespoon Mr. Boston Coffee Flavored Brandy
1 teaspoon vanilla
¾ cup flour
Confectioners' sugar
Creamy Coffee Filling (see below)
½ cup chopped walnuts

Beat together egg yolks and sugar until thick and lemon-colored. Stir brandy and vanilla into yolk mixture. Beat egg whites until stiff, but not dry, peaks form; fold into yolk mixture. Sift flour over egg mixture and gently fold in. Spread batter in greased and wax paper-lined 15½x10½-inch jelly-roll pan. Bake in preheated 400°F. oven 10–15 minutes or until lightly browned. Immediately turn onto clean towel that has been heavily dusted with confectioners' sugar. Remove wax paper. Beginning at narrow end, roll up jelly-roll fashion. Cool completely. Unroll cake and spread with Creamy Coffee Filling. Sprinkle with nuts. Re-roll without towel and dust with confectioners' sugar.

10–12 servings

Creamy Coffee Filling

¾ cup butter
1½ cups confectioners' sugar
3 tablespoons Mr. Boston Coffee Flavored Brandy

Beat together butter and sugar until light and fluffy. Blend in brandy.

SUN-SPARKLED CAKE

Beat egg whites until foamy. Gradually add ½ cup sugar and beat until stiff, but not dry, peaks form; set aside. Beat 6 egg yolks and ½ cup sugar until thick and lemon-colored. Blend in 1½ teaspoons grated peel and 2 tablespoons Mandarine Napoleon. Gently fold into egg whites. Sift flour and baking powder, sprinkle over egg mixture, and gently fold in. Pour batter into three greased and wax paper-lined 8-inch round pans. Bake in preheated 375°F. oven 35–40 minutes or until cake springs back when lightly touched. Remove from pans and cool completely. Combine pudding mix and ¼ cup sugar in saucepan. Blend in water and 3 tablespoons Mandarine Napoleon and cook, stirring constantly, until mixture boils. Boil 1 minute. Remove from heat and allow to cool completely. Just before assembling cake, beat cream, together with remaining 3 tablespoons Mandarine Napoleon and 1½ teaspoons grated peel, until stiff. Spread bottom cake layer with half the lemon filling. Top with second layer and remaining lemon filling. Top with third layer and whipped cream. Refrigerate until ready to serve.

three 8-inch round layers

6 eggs, separated
1¼ cups sugar
½ cup Mandarine Napoleon
1 tablespoon grated tangerine or orange peel
1 cup flour
1 teaspoon baking powder
1 three-and-three-quarter-ounce package non-instant lemon pudding and pie filling
1¾ cups water
½ cup heavy cream

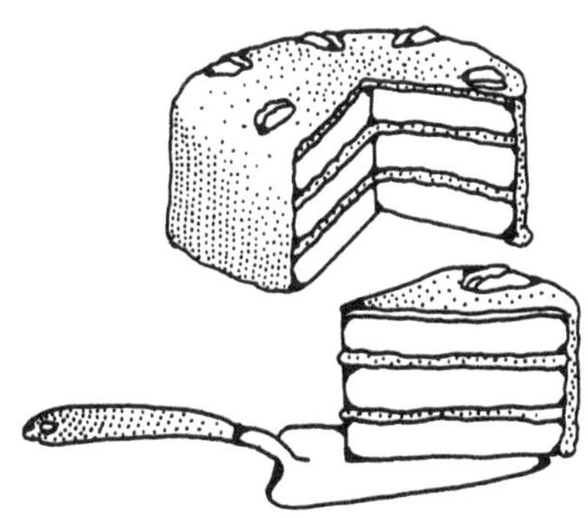

CHOCOLATE RASPBERRY CAKE

1 cup butter
2 cups sugar
4 squares (4 ounces) unsweetened chocolate, melted
4 eggs
2½ cups flour
2 teaspoons baking powder
1 teaspoon baking soda
1 teaspoon salt
¾ cup buttermilk
7 tablespoons Mr. Boston Crème de Cassis
2 tablespoons cornstarch
¼ cup water
2 ten-ounce packages frozen raspberries, thawed and drained; reserve ⅔ cup syrup
1½ cups heavy cream
¼ cup confectioners' sugar

Beat together butter and sugar until light and fluffy. Beat in melted chocolate and eggs, one at a time, beating well after each addition. Stir together flour, baking powder, baking soda, and salt. Blend buttermilk and ¼ cup crème de cassis. Alternately blend flour mixture and milk mixture into creamed mixture, beginning and ending with flour. Pour batter into three greased and wax paper-lined 8-inch round pans. Bake in preheated 350°F. oven 30–40 minutes. Cool 10 minutes; remove from pans and cool completely. Combine cornstarch and water. Add reserved syrup and bring to a boil; reduce heat and cook, stirring constantly, until thickened. Remove from heat, stir in raspberries and 2 tablespoons crème de cassis, and allow to cool. Spread half the raspberry mixture over bottom two layers. Beat cream with sugar and remaining 1 tablespoon crème de cassis until stiff. Frost top and sides of cake with whipped cream.

three 8-inch round layers

BRANDIED DARK FRUITCAKE

Soak fruits in brandy overnight. Add nuts. Mix 1 cup of the flour with fruits and nuts. Stir together remaining 1 cup flour, soda, and spices. Beat together butter and sugar until light and fluffy. Stir in flour mixture. Pour over fruit-nut mixture, stirring gently until well mixed. Pour into greased and brown paper-lined 10-inch tube pan. Bake in preheated 275°F. oven 3¼ hours. If desired, glaze fruitcake with hot corn syrup. Let age 2 weeks or longer.

one 7-pound cake

2½ cups (1 pound) chopped, pitted dates
2 cups candied cherries
1 cup mixed candied fruit
1 cup dark raisins
1 cup Mr. Boston Five Star Brandy
2 cups (½ pound) pecan halves
2 cups flour
½ teaspoon baking soda
½ teaspoon mace
½ teaspoon cloves
½ teaspoon cinnamon
½ cup butter
1 cup sugar
3 eggs
Corn syrup (optional)

ORANGE BLOSSOM CAKE

¾ cup butter, softened
1½ cups sugar
3 eggs
3 cups flour
1½ tablespoons baking powder
1½ teaspoons salt
½ cup milk
¼ cup orange juice
¼ cup Mr. Boston Triple Sec
1 tablespoon grated orange peel
Orange Frosting (see below)

Beat together butter and sugar until light and fluffy. Add eggs, one at a time, beating well after each addition. Stir together flour, baking powder, and salt. Blend milk, orange juice, triple sec, and orange peel. Alternately blend flour mixture and milk mixture into creamed mixture, beginning and ending with flour. Pour into two greased and floured or wax paper-lined 9-inch round pans or one 9x13-inch pan. Bake in preheated 350°F. oven 25–35 minutes for layers, 40–45 minutes for sheet, or until golden brown. Cool 10 minutes before removing from pans. Cool completely and frost with Orange Frosting.

two 9-inch round layers or one 9x13-inch sheet cake

Orange Frosting

½ cup butter, softened
6 cups confectioners' sugar
2 tablespoons Mr. Boston Triple Sec
1 tablespoon grated orange peel
½ teaspoon salt
⅓–½ cup milk

Beat butter until light and fluffy; gradually add 1 cup sugar, beating until smooth. Add triple sec, orange peel, salt, and 2 tablespoons milk; beat until smooth and creamy. Gradually add remaining sugar. Add more milk as needed to attain spreading consistency.

MOCHA POUND CAKE

Beat together butter and sugar until light and fluffy. Add eggs, one at a time, beating well after each addition. Stir together flour, baking powder, and salt. Combine brandy, milk, chocolate, and vanilla in saucepan; heat until chocolate is melted. Alternately blend flour mixture and liquid into creamed mixture, beginning and ending with flour. Beat 2 minutes after all flour is blended into batter. Pour into greased and floured 9- or 10-inch tube pan. Bake in preheated 350°F. oven 45–55 minutes or until wooden pick inserted near center comes out clean. Cool 10 minutes in pan. Remove from pan and cool. Frost top with Creamy Chocolate Glaze.

one 9- or 10-inch round cake

¾ cup butter, softened
1¼ cups sugar
3 eggs
2½ cups flour
1 tablespoon baking powder
1 teaspoon salt
⅓ cup Mr. Boston Coffee Flavored Brandy
¼ cup milk
1 one-ounce square semi-sweet chocolate
1 teaspoon vanilla
Creamy Chocolate Glaze (see below)

Creamy Chocolate Glaze

Beat together cream cheese, chocolate, and sugar until smooth. Add enough crème de cacao to attain desired consistency. Spread over cooled cake.

1 three-ounce package cream cheese, softened
1 one-ounce square semi-sweet chocolate, melted
2 tablespoons confectioners' sugar
1–2 tablespoons Mr. Boston Crème de Cacao

BRANDIED PEACH SHORTCAKES WITH PEACH BRANDY CREAM

6 peaches (1½–2 pounds) peeled and sliced
¼ cup confectioners' sugar
½ cup Mr. Boston Peach Flavored Brandy
2 cups flour
1 tablespoon baking powder
2 tablespoons sugar
½ teaspoon salt
½ cup butter
1 egg
¼–½ cup milk
Butter, softened
Peach Brandy Cream (see below)

Sprinkle peaches with confectioners' sugar and brandy. Toss until each peach is evenly coated; let stand 1 hour. Stir together flour, baking powder, sugar, and salt. Cut in butter until mixture resembles coarse crumbs. Blend egg and ¼ cup milk; stir into flour mixture and blend until flour is moistened. Add more milk if needed to make soft dough. Knead on lightly floured surface 30 seconds. Roll out to ½-inch thickness. Cut into 6 rounds with floured 3-inch cutter. Place rounds on greased baking sheet. Bake in preheated 450°F. oven 10–12 minutes. Split biscuits while warm. Spread with softened butter. Spoon peaches and juice over bottoms and tops with Peach Brandy Cream. Replace tops. Garnish with a dollop of Peach Brandy Cream and a peach slice.

6 servings

Peach Brandy Cream

½ cup heavy cream
1 tablespoon confectioners' sugar
1–2 tablespoons Mr. Boston Peach Flavored Brandy

Whip cream with sugar until stiff. Blend in brandy.

Ice Cream Bombe & Blackberry Brandy Sauce

Peppermint Schnapps Parfaits

Mr. BOSTON
True Fruit Flavors
Mr. BOSTON
BLACKBERRY
FLAVORED
BRANDY
SEVENTY PROOF · CARAMEL ADDED

PEPPERMINT
SCHNAPPS
The delightful flavor of this product is derived from fresh mint blended to perfection.
Perfect for a Peppermint Freeze
A delicious Liqueur, served at room temperature or on the rocks.
Mr. BOSTON
FIFTY FOUR PROOF • PRODUCED BY MR. BOSTON DISTILLER
BOSTON, MA, OWENSBORO, KY, ALBANY, GA.

CHERRY-CHOCOLATE TORTE

Beat together egg yolks, crème de cacao, and ¾ cup sugar until thick and lemon-colored. Stir together bread crumbs, cocoa, flour, and almonds; fold into egg-yolk mixture. Beat egg whites until foamy, gradually add ¼ cup sugar and salt, and beat until stiff, but not dry, peaks form. Fold egg-yolk mixture into egg whites. Pour batter into 3 greased and wax paper-lined 8-inch round pans. Bake in preheated 350°F. oven 25–30 minutes or until cake springs back when lightly pressed. Cool slightly, remove from pans, and cool completely. Bring water and remaining ¾ cup sugar to a boil, stirring until sugar is completely dissolved. Boil over medium-high heat 8–10 minutes. Remove from heat, cool to lukewarm, and stir in ¼ cup brandy and cinnamon. Prick cake layers and pour syrup evenly over top. Let stand 5–10 minutes. Whip cream until stiff. Blend in confectioners' sugar and remaining 2 tablespoons brandy. Spread whipped cream mixture over bottom layer; top with half the cherries. Repeat with second layer. Place third layer on top; frost top and sides with remaining cream. Decorate with chocolate curls. Refrigerate until ready to serve.

three 8-inch round layers

8 eggs, separated
2 tablespoons Mr. Boston Crème de Cacao (white)
1¾ cups sugar
⅔ cup fine, dry bread crumbs
½ cup cocoa
½ cup sifted flour
½ cup ground almonds
⅛ teaspoon salt
1 cup water
6 tablespoons Mr. Boston Cherry Flavored Brandy
½ teaspoon cinnamon
2 cups heavy cream
¼ cup confectioners' sugar
1 sixteen-ounce can sour red cherries, drained and rinsed
Chocolate curls

RUM-WALNUT TORTE

- 6 eggs, separated
- ¼ cup water
- 2 tablespoons Mr. Boston Virgin Islands Dark Rum
- 1 teaspoon vanilla
- 1½ cups sugar
- 2 cups fine, dry bread crumbs
- 1 cup ground walnuts
- 1 tablespoon baking powder
- Rum Butter Cream (see below)

Beat together egg yolks, water, rum, and vanilla until frothy. Add 1 cup sugar and beat until thick and lemon-colored. Stir together bread crumbs, nuts, and baking powder; blend into egg-yolk mixture. Beat egg whites until foamy; gradually add ½ cup sugar, beating until stiff, but not dry, peaks form. Fold egg whites into batter. Pour batter into two greased and wax paper-lined 8-inch round pans. Bake in preheated 350°F. oven 30–35 minutes, or until cake springs back when lightly pressed. Cool cake 15 minutes in pans; remove. Cool completely, and split each layer in half. Assemble torte on serving plate, spreading ¼ Rum Butter Cream between each layer and on top. Store in refrigerator.

two 8-inch round layers

Rum Butter Cream

- 1 cup plus 2 tablespoons milk
- ½ cup Mr. Boston Virgin Islands Dark Rum
- 6 tablespoons flour
- 1½ cups butter, softened
- 1½ cups sugar

Blend milk, rum, and flour in saucepan until smooth. Cook over medium-low heat until thickened, stirring constantly. Remove from heat, and cool to room temperature. Beat together butter and sugar until light and fluffy. Gradually beat in cooled flour mixture. If filling is too thin to spread, chill to thicken.

ALMOND TORTE

Beat egg yolks with 6 tablespoons sugar until thick and lemon-colored. Gradually beat in brandy. Beat egg whites until foamy, gradually add remaining sugar, and beat until stiff, but not dry, peaks form. Fold egg-yolk mixture, almonds, and flour into egg-white mixture. Pour into two greased and wax paper-lined 8-inch round pans. Bake in preheated 325°F. oven 20–25 minutes or until cake springs back when lightly pressed. Cool slightly before removing from pans. Cool completely. Frost with Chocolate Apricot Glaze.

two 8-inch round layers

6 eggs, separated
¾ cup sugar
¼ cup Mr. Boston Apricot Flavored Brandy
1 cup ground almonds
½ cup flour
Chocolate Apricot Glaze (see below)

Chocolate Apricot Glaze

Melt chocolate and butter over low heat. Blend in brandy and sugar until smooth and creamy. Spread between layers and over top of cake.

1 one-ounce square unsweetened chocolate
1 tablespoon butter
2 tablespoons Mr. Boston Apricot Flavored Brandy
2–3 cups confectioners' sugar

STRAWBERRY CROWN TORTE

1 cup butter, softened
4 cups confectioners' sugar
5 eggs
3 cups flour
2 teaspoons baking powder
1 cup milk
¼ cup Amaretto di Saronno
1 fifteen-ounce carton ricotta cheese
2 tablespoons cocoa
1 tablespoon Mr. Boston Crème de Cacao
½ cup strawberry preserves
Chocolate Frosting (see below)
10–12 whole strawberries

Beat together butter and sugar until light and fluffy. Add eggs, one at a time, beating well after each addition. Stir together flour and baking powder. Combine milk and 2 tablespoons Amaretto di Saronno. Blend flour mixture alternately with milk into creamed mixture, beginning and ending with flour. Pour into three greased and wax paper-lined 8-inch round pans. Bake in preheated 350°F. oven 35–40 minutes or until golden brown. Cool 10 minutes before removing from pans. Cool thoroughly on wire racks. Split each layer in half. Blend ⅔ cup ricotta cheese with cocoa and crème de cacao. Combine remaining ricotta cheese with preserves and remaining 2 tablespoons Amaretto di Saronno. Spread about ⅓ cup strawberry mixture between first two layers. Spread half the chocolate mixture between next two layers. Alternate fillings, ending with strawberry. Frost with Chocolate Frosting. Garnish with whole berries.

three 8-inch round layers

Chocolate Frosting

¼ cup plus 2 tablespoons butter
3 one-ounce squares unsweetened chocolate
¼ teaspoon salt
4 cups confectioners' sugar
4 tablespoons Mr. Boston Crème de Cacao
2–3 tablespoons milk

Melt 2 tablespoons butter and chocolate in saucepan. Beat remaining butter with 1 cup of sugar until light and fluffy; add melted chocolate. Blend in remaining sugar and crème de cacao. Add milk as needed to reach spreading consistency.

Cookies

These traditional little snacks assume an aura of sophistication when spirits are added to the batter or the topping. Gingersnaps and butter cookies, pinwheels, and nutballs become important enough to come to the table as the main dessert at an elegant meal. And what a wonderful gift they make, packed in tins. Lift the lid and the fragrance of rum or anisette, cherry brandy or bourbon wafts into the air. Try the cookie recipes here, then go on to make your favorites even better à la Mr. Boston.

FRUIT-FILLED PINWHEELS

Stir together flour, salt, baking soda, and nuts. Beat together butter and sugar until light and fluffy. Add egg and vanilla; beat until smooth. Gradually beat in flour mixture. Refrigerate dough until stiff, at least two hours. Divide dough in half. On piece of waxed paper, roll half of dough out to an 8-inch square. Spread half of Fruit Filling over dough. Roll up jelly-roll fashion. Wrap in waxed paper or plastic wrap. Repeat with remaining half of dough. Freeze several hours or overnight. Remove from freezer and thaw 10 minutes. Cut into slices about ⅛-inch thick. Place on lightly greased baking sheet and bake in preheated 375°F. oven 12–15 minutes or until lightly browned.

6 dozen pinwheels

2 cups flour
½ teaspoon salt
¼ teaspoon baking soda
½ cup finely chopped nuts
½ cup butter, softened
¾ cup brown sugar, firmly packed
1 egg
1 teaspoon vanilla extract
Fruit Filling (see below)

Fruit Filling

Combine all ingredients in saucepan; bring to a boil, reduce heat, and simmer 15 minutes or until excess liquid has evaporated. Cover and refrigerate until ready to use.

1½ cups chopped pitted dates
¾ cup water
½ cup chopped candied or maraschino cherries
¼ cup Mr. Boston Cherry Flavored Brandy

AMARETTO LACE COOKIES

- ½ cup Amaretto di Saronno
- ½ cup butter
- ⅔ cup dark brown sugar, firmly packed
- 1 cup chopped pecans
- ½ cup flour

Combine Amaretto di Saronno, butter, and sugar in saucepan; bring to a boil. Remove from heat, stir in pecans and flour, and beat well. Drop mixture by level tablespoonfuls four inches apart onto greased baking sheet. Bake in preheated 375°F. oven 6–8 minutes, or until deep brown and bubbly. Cool cookies on sheet 1 minute, then remove and immediately roll up like jelly rolls.

3 dozen cookies

STRAWBERRY GINGER BARS

- 2 cups all-purpose flour
- 1 cup whole wheat flour
- ⅓ cup sugar
- ½ teaspoon baking soda
- ½ teaspoon salt
- ¾ cup butter, softened
- 2 three-ounce packages cream cheese, softened
- 3 tablespoons Mr. Boston Ginger Flavored Brandy
- 2 teaspoons grated lemon peel
- 1 cup strawberry preserves
- ½ cup finely chopped nuts

Stir together flours, sugar, soda, and salt. Beat together butter, cream cheese, 1 tablespoon brandy, and lemon peel until light and fluffy. Knead flour mixture into creamed mixture. Divide dough into quarters; set two quarters aside. Pat each remaining quarter evenly over bottom of 8-inch square pan. Mix preserves with remaining 2 tablespoons brandy and spread half of mixture into each pan. Sprinkle with nuts. Roll each reserved quarter into an 8-inch square, cut into strips, and lattice over preserves. Bake in preheated 350°F. oven 35–40 minutes or until done. Cool thoroughly and cut into 2-inch bars.

32 bars

SWEDISH ALMOND CRISPS

Beat together butter and sugar until light and fluffy. Add egg and beat well. Stir in Amaretto di Saronno and almonds. Stir together flour and salt; gradually work flour mixture into creamed mixture. Form dough into 2 rolls about 10 inches long. Cover and refrigerate until stiff, 2–3 hours. Cut rolls into slices ⅛- to ¼-inch thick and place on greased baking sheets. Bake in preheated 350°F. oven 10 minutes or until lightly browned. Remove from baking sheets immediately. Cool on wire rack.

7 dozen cookies

1 cup butter, softened
1 cup sugar
1 egg
¼ cup Amaretto di Saronno
1 cup ground almonds
3 cups flour
1 teaspoon salt

BOURBON BALLS

Stir together dry ingredients. Blend bourbon and corn syrup and add to dry ingredients. Mix by hand until mixture holds its shape. Shape into 1-inch balls and roll in confectioners' sugar. Age in air-tight container at least one week before serving.

2 dozen balls

1 cup vanilla wafer crumbs
1 cup finely chopped pecans
1 cup sifted confectioners' sugar
2 tablespoons cocoa
¼ cup Yellowstone Mellow Mash
1½ tablespoons light corn syrup
Confectioners' sugar

FENNEL CAKES

- 1 cup butter, softened
- 1½ cups sugar
- 2 teaspoons fennel seeds
- 1 teaspoon grated lemon peel
- 2 tablespoons Mr. Boston Anisette
- 2 cups flour
- 1 teaspoon baking powder
- ½ teaspoon salt
- ½ cup chopped pistachio nuts (optional)

Beat together butter and sugar until light and fluffy. Add fennel seeds, lemon peel, and anisette. Stir together flour, baking powder, and salt. Blend flour mixture and nuts into creamed mixture to make a stiff dough. Refrigerate until firm. Form dough into small balls about ¾-inch in diameter. Place on greased baking sheets. Bake in preheated 350°F. oven 10–12 minutes or until lightly browned. Cool slightly on baking sheet before removing. Cool completely on wire rack.

5 dozen cakes

LEMON SUGAR COOKIES

- 1 cup butter, softened
- 1 cup sugar
- 3 tablespoons lemon juice
- 1 tablespoon grated lemon peel
- 2 tablespoons Amaretto di Saronno
- 2½ cups flour
- 2 teaspoons baking powder
- ½ teaspoon salt
- Sugar

Beat together butter and sugar until light and fluffy. Add lemon juice, peel, and Amaretto di Saronno; blend thoroughly. Stir together flour, baking powder, and salt; add to creamed mixture and blend well. Chill 2–3 hours. Shape rounded teaspoons of dough into balls. Roll in sugar and place on ungreased baking sheet 2 inches apart. Flatten each with a glass bottom. Bake in preheated 350°F. oven 12–14 minutes or until golden brown.

5 dozen cookies

ORANGE CHOCOLATE CHIP COOKIES

Beat together butter and sugar until light and fluffy. Beat in egg, orange peel, and triple sec. Stir together flour, baking powder, and salt; blend into creamed mixture. Stir in chocolate chips and nuts. Drop by level tablespoonfuls onto greased baking sheets. Bake in preheated 375°F. oven 10–12 minutes.

4½ dozen cookies

- **⅔ cup butter, softened**
- **1 cup dark brown sugar, firmly packed**
- **1 egg**
- **¼ cup grated orange peel**
- **2 tablespoons Mr. Boston Triple Sec**
- **2¼ cups flour**
- **½ teaspoon baking powder**
- **1 teaspoon salt**
- **1 cup mini chocolate chips**
- **½ cup chopped walnuts**

BRANDIED GINGERSNAPS

Beat together shortening and brown sugar until light and fluffy. Combine molasses and ginger brandy; add to creamed mixture with egg. Beat until well blended. Stir together dry ingredients; add to molasses mixture; blend well. Refrigerate dough for several hours or overnight. Form into small balls. Roll in sugar. Place 2 inches apart on greased baking sheet. Bake in preheated 375°F. oven about 10 minutes. Remove from pan immediately.

5 dozen cookies

- **¾ cup shortening**
- **1 cup light brown sugar, firmly packed**
- **¼ cup molasses**
- **2 tablespoons Mr. Boston Ginger Flavored Brandy**
- **1 egg**
- **2¼ cups flour**
- **2 teaspoons baking soda**
- **½ teaspoon salt**
- **½ teaspoon cinnamon**
- **½ teaspoon ground cloves**
- **Sugar**

MINTED BUTTER COOKIES

1 cup butter, softened
¾ cup sugar
3 tablespoons Mr. Boston Crème de Menthe (white)
2¼ cups flour
¼ teaspoon salt
1 tablespoon butter
½ one-ounce square unsweetened chocolate
¼ cup confectioners' sugar

Beat together butter and sugar until light and fluffy. Add 2 tablespoons crème de menthe and flour; blend well. Refrigerate until stiff. Shape into 1-inch balls. Place on ungreased baking sheet 2 inches apart. Bake in preheated 400°F. oven 10–12 minutes or until set. While cookies are still warm, make depression in center with thimble or spoon handle. Melt butter and chocolate. Stir in sugar. Beat in remaining 1 tablespoon crème de menthe. Place ¼–½ teaspoon chocolate mixture in center of each cookie. Cool until firm.

4 dozen cookies

ORANGE CARAWAY COOKIES

½ cup butter, softened
1 cup sugar
1 egg
2 tablespoons Mr. Boston Triple Sec
1 teaspoon caraway seeds
2½ cups flour
¼ teaspoon baking soda
½ teaspoon salt

Beat together butter and sugar until light and fluffy. Add egg, triple sec, and caraway and beat until smooth. Stir together dry ingredients and blend into creamed mixture. Shape into roll 2 inches in diameter and chill until firm. Cut into ¼-inch slices. Place on greased baking sheets and bake in preheated 400°F. oven 8–10 minutes.

4 dozen cookies

MOCHA NUT BALLS

Beat together butter, sugar, and brandy until light and fluffy. Add remaining ingredients and mix well. Shape into 1-inch balls and place on ungreased baking sheets 1½ inches apart. Bake in preheated 325°F. oven 15–18 minutes. Cool and roll in confectioners' sugar.

5 dozen balls

1 cup butter, softened
½ cup light brown sugar, firmly packed
3 tablespoons Mr. Boston Coffee Flavored Brandy
⅓ cup cocoa
1½ cups flour
½ teaspoon salt
2 cups finely chopped walnuts
Confectioners' sugar

CRESCENT COOKIES

Beat together butter, sugar, and oil until light and fluffy. Add eggs, one at a time, beating well after each addition. Stir together flour and baking powder. Blend sour mash and milk. Alternately blend flour mixture and liquid mixture into creamed mixture, beginning and ending with flour mixture, to make a soft dough. Divide dough into sixths. Roll each portion on a lightly floured surface to an 8-inch circle; cut each circle into 6 wedges. Roll up each wedge, beginning with long end and rolling toward point. Shape into crescent and place on greased baking sheet. Brush with egg white and bake in preheated 350°F. oven 20–25 minutes or until lightly browned.

3 dozen cookies

1 cup butter, softened
½ cup sugar
¼ cup oil
2 eggs
3½ cups flour
1½ teaspoons baking powder
2 tablespoons Yellowstone Mellow Mash
2 tablespoons milk
1 egg white, beaten

ITALIAN ANISE BISCOTTI

- **½ cup butter, softened**
- **1 cup sugar**
- **1½ tablespoons anise seed**
- **3 eggs**
- **2 tablespoons Mr. Boston Triple Sec**
- **1 teaspoon vanilla**
- **2½ cups flour**
- **1½ teaspoons baking powder**
- **1 cup chopped almonds, optional**

Beat together butter and sugar until light and fluffy. Add anise seed, eggs, and liquid; beat thoroughly. Stir together flour and baking powder; blend into creamed mixture. Stir in nuts. Chill dough until firm, about 1½ hours. Divide dough in half; shape each half on lightly floured surface to flat loaf about 2 inches wide and ½-inch thick. Place loaves six inches apart on a large greased baking sheet. Bake in preheated 375°F. oven 20 minutes. Remove from oven and cool 5 minutes. Cut loaves into diagonal slices ½-inch thick. Place slices on baking sheet. Return to oven and bake another 12–15 minutes, or until lightly toasted.

4 dozen biscuits

BRANDIED RAISIN BARS

- **2½ cups dark raisins**
- **1 cup water**
- **1 cup Mr. Boston Five Star Brandy**
- **½ cup butter, softened**
- **1 cup sugar**
- **2 eggs**
- **3 cups flour**
- **1½ tablespoons baking powder**
- **1½ teaspoons salt**
- **1 teaspoon cinnamon**
- **1 teaspoon nutmeg**
- **1 teaspoon mace**
- **1 cup chopped nuts, optional**

Simmer raisins in water and brandy 15 minutes; cool 15–20 minutes. Beat together butter and sugar until light and fluffy. Beat in eggs. Add raisin mixture. Stir together flour, baking powder, salt, and spices; blend into creamed mixture. Stir in nuts. Spread batter into greased 15½x10½-inch jelly roll pan. Bake in preheated 325°F. oven 30 minutes. Cool 10 minutes before removing from pan. Cut into 2x3-inch bars.

25 bars

KENTUCKY BOURBON FRUIT COOKIES

Soak cherries and raisins in bourbon for 1 hour. Beat together butter and sugar until light and fluffy. Add eggs and beat well. Stir in fruits and pecans. Stir together flour, baking powder, soda, salt, and spices; blend into fruit mixture. Drop by rounded tablespoonfuls onto greased baking sheet. Bake in preheated 350°F. oven 15–18 minutes.

5 dozen cookies

- **1 pound candied cherries, coarsely chopped**
- **2½ cups raisins**
- **¾ cup Old Kentucky Tavern Straight Bourbon Whiskey**
- **½ cup butter, softened**
- **½ cup light brown sugar, packed**
- **2 eggs**
- **3 cups chopped pecans**
- **2 cups flour**
- **1 tablespoon baking powder**
- **1½ teaspoons baking soda**
- **1 teaspoon salt**
- **1 teaspoon cinnamon**
- **1 teaspoon nutmeg**
- **½ teaspoon ground cloves**

Mocha Cheesecake Saronno

Brandied Peach Shortcakes with Peach Brandy Cream

ILLVA
AMARETTO
di
SARONNO
ORIGINALE
A LIQUEUR PRODUCED BY
ILLVA SARONNO ITALY

True Fruit Flavors
Mr. BOSTON
PEACH
FLAVORED
BRANDY

Pastries

There are many ways to introduce a spirited accent into pastries, pies, and tarts: blend brandy into the crust, beat Mandarine Napoleon into the cream cheese filling, whip crème de menthe into the cream topping. Your favorite pie recipes will benefit by the addition of just the right cordial. And what better way to transform your favorite cocktail into a meal-capping climax than to serve it as a dessert? A Marguerita becomes a pie, and a Brandy Alexander becomes a tartlet.

NESSELRODE PIE

For the crust:
- 2 cups flour
- 1 teaspoon salt
- ⅔ cup shortening
- 4–8 tablespoons cold water

Stir together flour and salt. Cut in shortening until mixture resembles coarse crumbs. Sprinkle with water, 1 to 2 tablespoons at a time, mixing lightly until dough forms a ball. Roll out on lightly floured surface to 12-inch circle and fit loosely into 10-inch deep-dish pie pan. Trim pastry and flute edges. Prick inside of shell with fork. Bake in preheated 400°F. oven 10–12 minutes or until golden brown.

For the filling:
- ⅓ cup sugar
- 3 tablespoons cornstarch
- 1 envelope (1 tablespoon) unflavored gelatin
- 3 eggs, separated
- 1½ cups milk
- ¼ cup Mr. Boston Virgin Islands Dark Rum
- 1 four-ounce bar sweet baking chocolate, finely chopped
- 1½ cups heavy cream, whipped
- ½ cup chopped maraschino cherries
- ½ cup chopped pecans

Combine sugar, cornstarch, gelatin, egg yolks, and milk in saucepan. Cook over medium heat, stirring constantly, until smooth and thickened. Measure out 1¼ cups of the mixture and chill until thickened. Add 2 tablespoons rum and 2 ounces chocolate to remaining mixture and cook until chocolate melts, stirring occasionally. Remove from heat and chill until thickened. Beat egg whites until stiff, but not dry, peaks form. Fold into chilled light mixture. Fold 1 cup whipped cream into chilled chocolate mixture and remaining whipped cream into light mixture. Stir cherries and nuts into light mixture. Spoon chocolate mixture into bottom of pie shell. Top with light mixture. Sprinkle with remaining 2 ounces chocolate. Cover and refrigerate until firm, 3–4 hours.

one 10-inch deep-dish pie

BANANA CREAM PIE

1½ cups vanilla wafer crumbs
¼ cup melted butter
⅔ cup sugar
¼ cup cornstarch
½ teaspoon salt
3 cups milk
4 egg yolks, beaten
2 tablespoons butter
¼ cup Mr. Boston Crème de Banana
2 bananas, sliced
Flavored Cream (see below)

Combine crumbs and butter; press over bottom and sides of 9-inch pie pan. Bake in preheated 350°F. oven 10 minutes. Mix sugar, cornstarch, and salt in saucepan. Gradually stir in milk. Cook over medium heat, stirring constantly, until mixture thickens. Stir half the hot mixture into egg yolks. Blend egg-yolk mixture back into remaining hot mixture. Bring to a boil and cook, stirring constantly, 1 minute. Remove from heat; stir in butter and crème de banana. Place bananas in bottom of pie shell. Pour mixture over top. Chill 2–3 hours or until firm. Top with Flavored Cream before serving.

one 9-inch pie

Flavored Cream

1 cup heavy cream
2 tablespoons sugar
2 tablespoons Mr. Boston Crème de Banana

Beat cream with other ingredients until stiff.

BANANA DAIQUIRI PIE

1¼ cups graham cracker crumbs
3 tablespoons sugar
¼ teaspoon cinnamon
⅓ cup melted butter
1½ tablespoons unflavored gelatin
½ cup cold water
¼ cup lime juice
3 tablespoons Mr. Boston Virgin Islands Light Rum
3 tablespoons Mr. Boston Crème de Banana
4 eggs, separated
½ cup sugar
Whipped cream

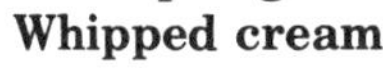

Combine crumbs, sugar, cinnamon, and butter; press over bottom and sides of 10-inch pie pan. Chill. Sprinkle gelatin over water in saucepan; let stand 5 minutes. Heat to a boil, remove from heat, and stir in lime juice, rum, and crème de banana; cool to room temperature. Beat egg yolks and ¼ cup sugar until thick and lemon-colored. Beat in cooled gelatin mixture. Chill, stirring often, until mixture thickens slightly. Beat egg whites until foamy. Gradually beat in remaining sugar until stiff, but not dry, peaks form. Fold egg whites into gelatin mixture. Spoon into prepared pie shell. Refrigerate until firm, at least 4 hours. Decorate top with lattice of whipped cream.

one 10-inch pie

CRANBERRY CASSIS PIE

2 cups flour
1 tablespoon grated orange peel
1 teaspoon salt
1 teaspoon nutmeg
½ cup shortening
½–¾ cup cold water
1 sixteen-ounce package cranberries
½ cup water
½ cup Mr. Boston Crème de Cassis
¼ cup cornstarch
¾ cup sugar

Stir together flour, orange peel, salt, and nutmeg. Cut in shortening until mixture resembles coarse crumbs. Add water, 1–2 tablespoons at a time, until dough forms ball. Divide dough in half. Roll half out to 11-inch circle. Fit into 9-inch pie pan. Cook cranberries in water until tender, 5–8 minutes. Drain. Blend crème de cassis and cornstarch; stir mixture into cranberries along with sugar. Cook over medium heat, stirring constantly, until mixture comes to a boil. Reduce heat and cook until thickened. Remove from heat and allow to cool slightly. Pour cooled mixture into prepared pie shell. Roll out remaining half of dough to 10-inch circle. Place over filling. Trim, seal, and flute edges. Cut several vent holes in top crust. Bake in preheated 400°F. oven 25–30 minutes or until crust is golden brown.

one 9-inch pie

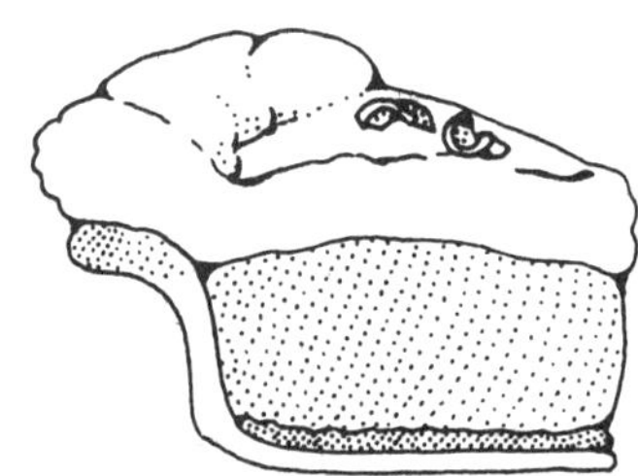

MARGUERITA PIE

Combine pretzel crumbs and butter. Press over bottom and sides of 9-inch pie pan. Bake in preheated 350°F. oven 10 minutes. Stir lime juice and peel, tequila, and triple sec into evaporated milk. Fold in whipped topping and pour entire mixture into pie shell. Freeze 3–4 hours or until firm. Let stand at room temperature 5 minutes before serving.

one 9-inch pie

- **1½ cups coarse pretzel crumbs**
- **6 tablespoons butter, melted**
- **3 tablespoons lime juice**
- **2 teaspoons grated lime peel**
- **5 tablespoons Gavilan Tequila**
- **3 tablespoons Mr. Boston Triple Sec**
- **1 thirteen-ounce can evaporated milk**
- **1½ cups prepared whipped topping**

MINT BROWNIE PIE

Beat together egg whites and salt until soft peaks form. Gradually add sugar, beating until stiff, but not dry, peaks form. Fold in ¼ cup crème de cacao, ¾ cup chocolate wafer crumbs, and nuts. Spread mixture in buttered 8-inch pie pan. Sprinkle with remaining chocolate wafer crumbs. Bake in preheated 325°F. oven 25–30 minutes or until firm. Cool completely. Whip cream until soft peaks form. Add crème de menthe and whip until stiff. Spread over pie.

one 8-inch pie

- **3 egg whites**
- **⅛ teaspoon salt**
- **½ cup sugar**
- **¼ cup Mr. Boston Crème de Cacao**
- **1 cup fine chocolate wafer crumbs**
- **½ cup coarsely chopped walnuts**
- **1 cup heavy cream**
- **2 tablespoons Mr. Boston Crème de Menthe (white)**

MANDARINE NAPOLEON MERINGUE PIE

For the crust:

1½ cups flour
1 teaspoon salt
½ cup shortening
3–6 tablespoons cold water

Stir together flour and salt. Cut in shortening until mixture resembles coarse crumbs. Sprinkle with water 1–2 tablespoons at a time, mixing lightly until dough forms a ball. Roll out on lightly floured surface to 11-inch circle and fit loosely into 9-inch pie pan. Trim pastry and flute edge. Prick inside with fork. Bake in preheated 400°F. oven 10–12 minutes or until golden brown.

For the filling:

1 cup plus 2 tablespoons sugar
¼ teaspoon salt
5 tablespoons cornstarch
1 cup water
3 eggs, separated
⅓ cup plus 1 tablespoon Mandarine Napoleon
2 teaspoons grated orange peel
2 tablespoons butter
1 tablespoon lemon juice

Mix together well ¾ cup sugar, salt, cornstarch, and ½ cup water in saucepan. Blend in remaining water; cook, stirring constantly, over low heat until mixture boils. Boil 1 minute and remove from heat. Beat egg yolks with ⅓ cup Mandarine Napoleon, orange peel, and butter; add to hot mixture, beating constantly. Return to heat and cook 1 minute longer. Stir in lemon juice. Cool 5 minutes, stirring twice while cooling. Pour mixture into prepared pie shell. Beat egg whites until foamy. Add remaining 1 tablespoon Mandarine Napoleon and remaining 6 tablespoons sugar, 1 tablespoon at a time. Beat until stiff, but not dry, peaks form. Spread meringue first around edge of filling so that it touches crust, then fill in center. Bake in preheated 425°F. oven 4–5 minutes to lightly brown meringue. Cool to room temperature and refrigerate.

one 9-inch pie

Note: This pie is at its best when it is made and served the same day.

SPIRITED PECAN PIE

Stir together flour and salt. Cut shortening into flour until mixture resembles coarse crumbs. Sprinkle with water, 1–2 tablespoons at a time, mixing lightly until dough forms a ball. Roll out on lightly floured surface to 11-inch circle and fit loosely into 9-inch pie pan. Trim pastry and flute edge. Beat eggs. Add all remaining ingredients except pecans; beat well. Stir in pecans. Pour into unbaked pie shell. Bake in preheated 350°F. oven 45–50 minutes.

one 9-inch pie

1½ cups flour
1 teaspoon salt
½ cup shortening
3–6 tablespoons cold water
3 eggs
1 cup dark corn syrup
⅔ cup sugar
¼ cup butter, melted
¼ cup Mr. Boston Virgin Islands Dark Rum
¼ teaspoon salt
1 cup pecan halves

STRAWBERRY CREAM PUFF RING

Combine butter and water in saucepan and bring to a boil. Add flour and salt, stirring constantly, 1–2 minutes, until mixture forms a ball. Remove from heat; cool slightly. Add eggs, one at a time, beating well after each addition. On lightly greased baking sheet, form dough into ring. Bake in preheated 400°F. oven 45–50 minutes or until browned. Remove from oven and cool thoroughly on wire rack. Slice enough strawberries to make 2 cups. Reserve remainder. Whip cream with sugar and cognac until stiff. Fold in sour cream and sliced berries. Cut top ⅓- to ½-inch off pastry ring. Scoop out center to form trench. Fill with strawberry mixture. Replace top. Place remaining berries in center of ring. Serve with any remaining strawberry mixture as topping.

8–10 servings

½ cup butter
1 cup water
1 cup flour
⅛ teaspoon salt
4 eggs
1 quart strawberries
1 cup heavy cream
3 tablespoons brown sugar
3 tablespoons Rémy Martin V.S.O.P. Cognac
½ cup sour cream

FRUIT FLAN

2 cups flour
7 tablespoons sugar
1 teaspoon salt
½ cup butter
¼ cup cold water
5 eggs
1 cup half-and-half, scalded
¼ cup Mr. Boston Triple Sec
½ teaspoon vanilla
1 eleven-ounce can mandarin orange sections, drained

Stir together flour, 3 tablespoons sugar, and salt. Cut in butter until mixture resembles coarse crumbs. Blend water and 1 egg until smooth. Stir into flour until mixture forms a ball. Chill 30 minutes. Roll out to 14-inch circle. Fit into 10-inch tart pan. Trim edges, prick bottom, and chill 30 minutes. Bake in preheated 375°F. oven 15 minutes. Blend hot half-and-half with triple sec and vanilla. Beat remaining 4 eggs with remaining 4 tablespoons sugar until smooth. Gradually blend half-and-half mixture into egg mixture. Stir in oranges. Pour into pre-baked shell and bake in preheated 400°F. oven until set, about 20 minutes. Serve warm or cold.

8 servings

CHEESE TARTS

⅓ cup butter
⅓ cup shortening
2 cups flour
⅔—¾ cup water
1 eight-ounce package cream cheese, softened
⅓ cup sugar
¾ cup heavy cream
¼ cup Mandarine Napoleon
½ teaspoon grated orange peel
3 eggs
1 twenty-one-ounce can cherry pie filling

Cut butter and shortening into flour until mixture resembles coarse crumbs. Blend in water until mixture forms ball. Divide dough into 12 small pieces. Roll each out to 4- or 5-inch circle. Fit into tart pan; flute edges. Beat together cream cheese and sugar until light and fluffy. Beat in cream, Mandarine Napoleon, and orange peel until mixture becomes thick. Add eggs, one at a time, beating well after each addition. Pour about ⅓ cup of cheese mixture into each tart shell. Bake in preheated 350°F. oven 30–35 minutes or until crust is golden brown. Cool tarts and top with cherry pie filling.

twelve 4-inch tarts

BRANDY ALEXANDER TARTLETS

Cut butter into flour until mixture resembles coarse crumbs. Blend in sour cream until mixture forms ball. Cover and refrigerate 4–6 hours. Roll chilled pastry out to ⅛-inch thickness. Cut with 3-inch round cutter into 24 rounds. Cut 1½-inch center out of each of 16 rounds. Place 8 uncut rounds on baking sheet. Cover each with 2 of the cut rounds. Brush with beaten egg and sprinkle with 2 tablespoons sugar. Bake in preheated 350°F. oven 25–30 minutes or until golden brown. Cool. Blend cream cheese, crème de cacao, brandy, and remaining 2 tablespoons sugar until smooth. Spoon mixture into tartlets and top each with one strawberry.

8 tartlets

1 cup butter, softened
1½ cups flour
½ cup sour cream
1 egg, beaten
¼ cup sugar
2 three-ounce packages cream cheese, softened
2 tablespoons Mr. Boston Crème de Cacao
1 tablespoon Mr. Boston Five Star Brandy
8 whole strawberries

CITRUS TART

Stir together flour and salt. Cut in shortening until mixture resembles coarse crumbs. Stir in water, 1–2 tablespoons at a time, until dough forms ball. Divide in half and roll half out to 12-inch circle. Fit into 10-inch pie pan. Blend juices, Mandarine Napoleon, sugar, and eggs until smooth. Pour into pie shell. Roll out remaining dough to 6x12-inch rectangle. Cut into ½-inch strips and form lattice over top of filling. Bake in preheated 400°F. oven 15 minutes. Reduce heat to 325°F. and continue baking 40–50 minutes, or until knife inserted near center comes out clean. Cool and chill before serving. Serve with whipped cream.

one 10-inch pie

2 cups flour
1 teaspoon salt
½ cup shortening
½–¾ cup cold water
½ cup lemon juice
½ cup lime juice
¼ cup Mandarine Napoleon
2 cups sugar
5 eggs
Whipped cream

GLAZED APPLE DUMPLINGS

2 cups flour
1 teaspoon salt
⅔ cup shortening
4–8 tablespoons cold water
¼ cup Mr. Boston Rock & Rye
½ cup light brown sugar, packed
2 tablespoons light corn syrup
4 medium baking apples, peeled and cored
2 tablespoons raisins
2 tablespoons chopped walnuts
1 tablespoon butter or margarine
Vanilla ice cream or sweetened whipped cream

Stir together flour and salt. Cut in shortening until mixture resembles coarse crumbs. Stir in water, 1–2 tablespoons at a time, until dough forms a ball. Chill. Heat together Rock & Rye, sugar, and corn syrup until sugar dissolves. Divide pastry dough into 4 parts. Roll each on floured surface to an 8-inch square; trim edges. Place apple in center of each square. Fill apple cores with raisins, walnuts, and 1 teaspoon Rock & Rye syrup. Top each apple with dot of butter. Moisten edges of pastry. Bring each corner of square to top of apple; pinch edges together to enclose apple completely. Place dumplings in greased 8-inch-square pan. Bake in preheated 400°F. oven 25 minutes, or until pastry is golden and apples are tender. Pour remaining syrup over dumplings; bake 5 minutes more. Serve warm with ice cream or whipped cream.

4 dumplings

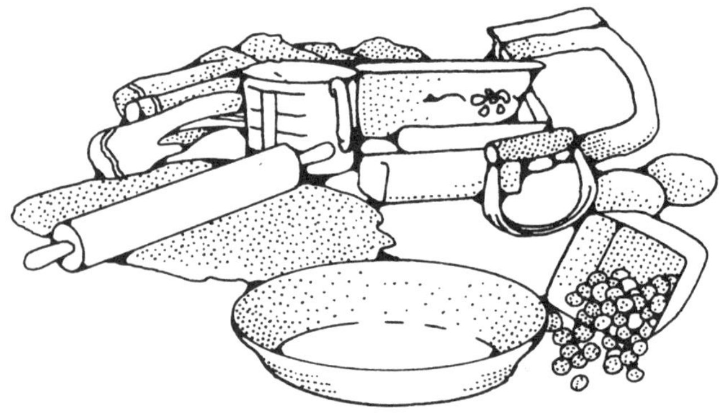

FLAKY PEACH DUMPLINGS

- **½ cup shortening**
- **3 cups flour**
- **½ cup Mr. Boston Peach Flavored Brandy**
- **½–¾ cup milk**
- **1 cup light brown sugar, packed**
- **1 teaspoon cinnamon**
- **½ teaspoon cloves**
- **½ teaspoon ginger**
- **½ cup butter, melted**
- **8 peaches, peeled, pitted, and halved**

Cut shortening into flour until mixture resembles coarse crumbs. Blend in ¼ cup peach brandy and enough milk to make soft dough. Turn onto lightly floured surface and knead gently 30 seconds. Divide dough in half. Roll each half out to a 12-inch square. Combine ⅔ cup brown sugar with spices. Brush each square with 2 tablespoons melted butter and sprinkle half the brown sugar mixture over each. Cut each 12-inch square into four 6-inch squares. Place 2 peach halves, cut sides together, in center of each square. Fold corners up to center, pinching to seal. Place in lightly greased 9x13-inch baking pan. Combine remaining butter, brown sugar, and peach brandy; pour over dumplings. Bake in preheated 400°F. oven 30–35 minutes, or until golden brown.

8 dumplings

PINK PEPPERMINT PIE

- **1½ cups chocolate wafer crumbs**
- **¼ cup melted butter**
- **24 large marshmallows**
- **½ cup milk**
- **¼ cup Mr. Boston Peppermint Schnapps**
- **⅛ teaspoon salt**
- **6 drops red food coloring**
- **1 cup heavy cream, whipped**
- **2 tablespoons crushed peppermint candy**

Combine crumbs and butter; press over bottom and sides of 9-inch pie pan. Bake in preheated 350°F. oven 10 minutes. Heat marshmallows and milk over low heat until marshmallows melt. Remove from heat. Stir in peppermint schnapps, salt, and food coloring. Refrigerate until thickened, stirring occasionally. Fold marshmallow mixture into whipped cream. Pour into pie shell and sprinkle with peppermint candy. Refrigerate until ready to serve.

one 9-inch pie

Coffee Cakes and Dessert Breads

There is enough adventure in the art of dessert breads to justify a special chapter for this alone. Dessert breads may be plain, sweetened, fruited, frosted, or fashioned into a myriad of shapes.

With the addition of spirits, all assume new and magical shadings of taste and fragrance. The professional and the novice alike will discover new versions of yeast breads, quick breads, loaf breads, coffee cakes—to be served either with meals or as the star attraction.

Banana Daiquiri Pie

Strawberry Cream Puff Ring

Brandy Alexander Tartlets

Coffeecakes Twist Saronno

CREME DE
Banana
fruit of bananas blended to perfection.
Mr. BOSTON

AMARETTO
di
SARONNO
ORIGINALE

HEARTY PEAR BREAD

Stir together dry ingredients. Combine yogurt, eggs, oil, and anisette. Add liquid ingredients all at once to flour mixture. Stir just until flour is moistened. Stir in pears. Pour batter into greased 4½x8½-inch loaf pan. Bake in preheated 350°F. oven 60–70 minutes or until cake tester comes out clean. Cover with foil tent during last 15 minutes of baking, if necessary, to prevent overbrowning.

1 loaf

2 cups flour
½ cup wheat germ
½ cup dark brown sugar, packed
1 tablespoon baking powder
1¼ teaspoons salt
¼ teaspoon ground coriander
1 eight-ounce carton lemon yogurt
2 eggs
⅓ cup oil
3 tablespoons Mr. Boston Anisette
1½ cups pears, cored, peeled, and chopped

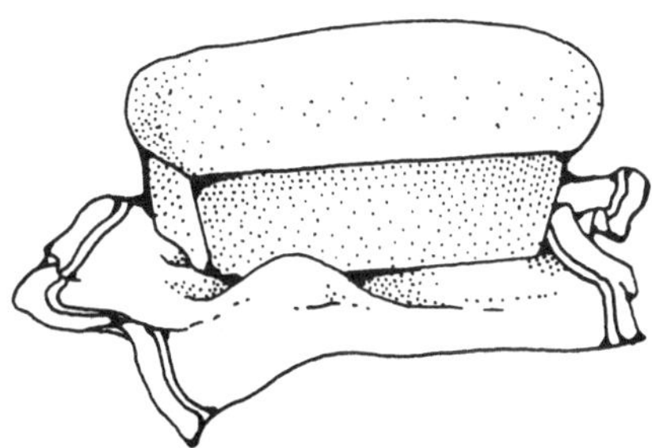

APPLESAUCE AND RAISIN BREAD

1 cup seedless raisins
¼ cup Mr. Boston Cherry Flavored Brandy
2 cups flour
1 tablespoon baking powder
1 teaspoon salt
1 teaspoon cinnamon
½ teaspoon ground cloves
1 cup applesauce
2 eggs, beaten
¼ cup dark brown sugar, packed
⅓ cup oil
½ cup chopped nuts (optional)

Soak raisins in brandy 10–15 minutes. Stir together flour, baking powder, salt, cinnamon, and cloves. Combine applesauce, eggs, sugar, and oil; stir in raisins and, if desired, nuts. Add all at once to flour, stirring only until flour is moistened. Pour into greased 4½x8½-inch loaf pan. Bake in preheated 350°F. oven 50–55 minutes or until done. Cool in pan 15 minutes before removing.

1 loaf

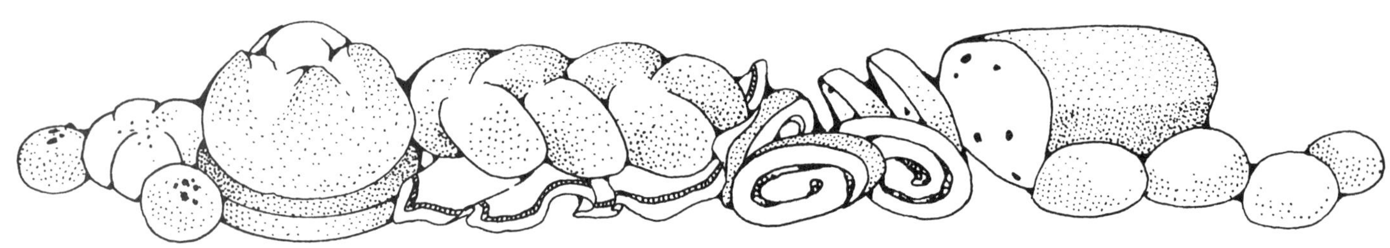

ORANGE NUT SWIRLS

½ cup sugar
½ cup light brown sugar, packed
1 tablespoon grated orange peel
¼ cup Mr. Boston Triple Sec
¼ cup orange juice
3 tablespoons butter
2 cups flour
1 tablespoon baking powder
1 teaspoon salt
¼ cup shortening
1 egg, beaten
½–¾ cup milk
¼ cup chopped nuts

Blend sugars and orange peel. Combine ¾ cup of the orange sugar with triple sec, orange juice, and 2 tablespoons butter in saucepan; bring to a boil. Reduce heat and continue to cook 5 minutes, stirring occasionally. Pour into 9-inch round cake pan. Stir together flour, baking powder, salt, and 2 tablespoons of the orange sugar. Cut in shortening until mixture resembles coarse crumbs. Stir in egg and enough milk to make soft dough. Knead gently on lightly floured surface 30 seconds. Roll out to a 10x12-inch rectangle. Melt remaining butter; brush over rectangle. Combine remaining orange sugar and nuts; sprinkle over dough. Roll up, beginning with 10-inch side, jelly-roll fashion. Cut into slices about 1-inch wide. Place cut side down in syrup in cake pan, with sides just touching. Bake in preheated 400°F. oven 20–25 minutes. Remove immediately from pan.

10–11 rolls

COFFEE CAKE TWIST SARONNO

4½–5 cups flour
2 packages dry yeast
1 cup milk
½ cup sugar
¼ cup butter
5–6 tablespoons Amaretto di Saronno
1 teaspoon salt
1 teaspoon grated orange peel
2 eggs, room temperature
½ cup finely chopped almonds
½ cup apricot preserves
1½ cups confectioners' sugar

Stir together 2 cups flour and yeast. Heat together milk, sugar, butter, 2 tablespoons Amaretto di Saronno, salt, and orange peel until very warm to touch (120°F.). Blend into flour mixture and beat until smooth. Blend in eggs. Add enough additional flour to make a moderately stiff dough. Knead on lightly floured surface until smooth and satiny, 8–10 minutes. Place dough in greased bowl and turn to grease all sides. Cover and let rise in warm place (80–85°F.) until doubled, about 1 hour. Punch down; let rest 10 minutes. Roll out to 10x16-inch rectangle. Mix almonds, preserves, and 1 tablespoon Amaretto di Saronno; spread mixture evenly over dough. Roll up like a jelly roll, starting at 16-inch side. Join ends of roll to form a ring and place on greased baking sheet. Cut with scissors at 1½-inch intervals, not quite all the way through. Let rise in warm place until doubled, about 45 minutes. Bake in preheated 350°F. oven 25–30 minutes or until deep golden brown. Mix confectioners' sugar with remaining 2–3 tablespoons Amaretto di Saronno to make glaze. Spoon over warm coffeecake, allowing glaze to run down sides.

one 12-inch ring

ALMOND BUBBLE COFFEE CAKE

4 cups flour
¼ cup sugar
½ cup butter
2 eggs
1⅓ cups milk
1 twelve-ounce can almond cake and pastry filling
3 tablespoons Amaretto di Saronno

Stir together flour and sugar. Cut in butter until mixture resembles coarse crumbs. Beat together eggs and milk; add to flour mixture and blend thoroughly. Knead gently on lightly floured surface 30 seconds. Divide dough in half. Roll each half out to a 10x12-inch rectangle. Combine almond filling and Amaretto di Saronno. Spread each rectangle with half the almond filling. Roll up jelly-roll fashion, beginning with long sides. Cut into 1-inch slices. Place slices on end in greased 9-inch square baking pan in three rows. Bake in preheated 450°F. oven 20–25 minutes or until golden brown. Remove from pan immediately.

one 9-inch square

SAVARIN

3½ cups flour
2 packages dry yeast
2 tablespoons sugar
1 cup warm water
6 eggs, room temperature
½ cup half-and-half
¾ cup butter, melted
1 teaspoon salt
Orange Almond Syrup (see below)
Sweetened whipped cream (optional)

Stir together 1 cup flour, yeast, and sugar. Add water and beat until smooth. Let rise in warm place (80–85°F.) until bubbly and doubled in bulk, about 1 hour. Stir down. Beat in eggs until smooth. Add cream and butter and beat until smooth. Stir in remaining flour and salt; blend until smooth. Cover and let rise in warm place until doubled in bulk, about 1 hour. Stir down. Pour into greased 10-inch bundt cake or fluted pan. Let rise in warm place until batter comes to top of pan. Bake in preheated 375°F. oven 35–40 minutes. Cool slightly in pan. Pierce with fork and pour Orange Almond Syrup over cake in pan. Cool and unmold. Serve with whipped cream, if desired.

one 10-inch cake

Orange Almond Syrup

¾ cup sugar
1½ cups water
⅓ cup Amaretto di Saronno
⅓ cup Mr. Boston Triple Sec
¼ cup Mr. Boston Virgin Islands Dark Rum

Combine sugar and water in saucepan, bring to a boil, and boil 15–20 minutes. Stir in liqueurs and rum and cook 5 minutes longer. Cool before pouring over cake.

PLUM COFFEE CAKE

Stir together flour, sugar, baking powder, and salt. Combine egg, ¼ cup reserved liquid, crème de cassis, and oil. Add liquid ingredients all at once to flour mixture, stirring only until flour is moistened. Stir in plums and nuts. Pour into greased 8-inch square pan. Sprinkle with Streusel Topping. Bake in preheated 375°F. oven 30–35 minutes or until wooden pick inserted near center comes out clean.

one 8-inch cake

- **1½ cups flour**
- **¼ cup sugar**
- **2 teaspoons baking powder**
- **¾ teaspoon salt**
- **1 egg, beaten**
- **1 sixteen-ounce can plums, packed in heavy syrup, drained and chopped; reserve liquid**
- **¼ cup Mr. Boston Crème de Cassis**
- **½ cup oil**
- **½ cup chopped nuts**
- **Streusel Topping (see below)**

Streusel Topping

Combine flour and sugar. Cut in butter until mixture resembles coarse crumbs. Distribute evenly over cake before baking.

- **¼ cup flour**
- **¼ cup light brown sugar, packed**
- **2 tablespoons butter, softened**

MORAVIAN SUGAR CAKE

2¼–2¾ cups flour
1 package dry yeast
3 tablespoons water
3 tablespoons Yellowstone Mellow Mash
¼ cup sugar
½ cup butter
½ teaspoon salt
1 egg
½ cup mashed potatoes (prepared instant may be used)
¼ cup brown sugar
1 teaspoon cinnamon

Stir together 1 cup flour and yeast. Heat water, mellow mash, sugar, ¼ cup butter, and salt until very warm to touch (120°F.). Add liquid ingredients to flour mixture and beat until smooth. Blend in egg and mashed potatoes. Add 1 cup flour and beat 1 minute. Stir in enough additional flour to make moderately stiff dough. Knead on lightly floured surface until smooth and satiny, 8–10 minutes. Shape into ball and place in lightly greased bowl, turning dough to grease all sides. Cover and let rise in warm place (80–85°F.) until doubled, about 1½ hours. Punch down. Let rest 10 minutes. Pat into 9x13-inch rectangle; fit into greased 9x13-inch pan. Mix brown sugar and cinnamon. Sprinkle over coffeecake. Melt remaining ¼ cup butter; drizzle over cake. Let rise in warm place until doubled, about 1 hour. Bake in preheated 350°F. oven 30–35 minutes. Remove from pan.

one 9x13-inch cake

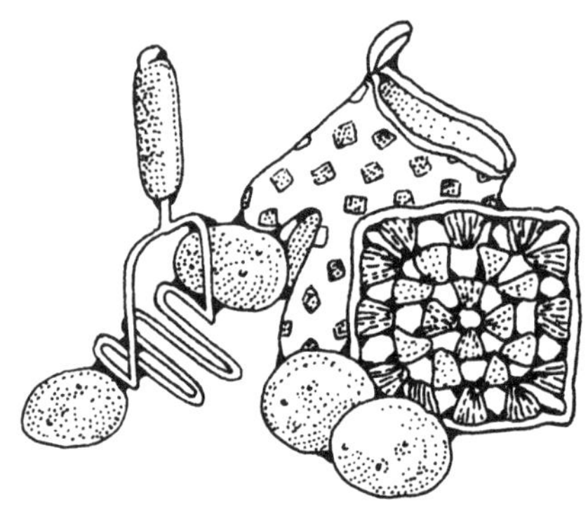

BLUEBERRY RIPPLE COFFEE CAKE

Combine all ingredients except blueberries and topping. Beat until smooth, 2–3 minutes. Spread half the batter in a greased 8-inch square pan. Cover with blueberries. Spread remaining batter over berries. Sprinkle with Streusel Topping. Bake in preheated 375°F. oven 35–40 minutes or until golden brown.

one 8-inch square cake

2 cups flour
½ cup sugar
1 tablespoon baking powder
1 teaspoon salt
½ teaspoon nutmeg
½ cup butter, softened
½ cup milk
3 tablespoons Mr. Boston Virgin Islands Dark Rum
1½ cups fresh or frozen blueberries
Streusel Topping (see below)

Streusel Topping

Stir together flour and sugar. Cut in butter until mixture resembles coarse crumbs. Distribute evenly over cake before baking.

¼ cup flour
¼ cup brown sugar
2 tablespoons butter, softened

RUM RAISIN BREAD

1½ cups raisins
6 tablespoons Mr. Boston Virgin Islands Rum
5½–6 cups flour
2 packages dry yeast
1 cup milk
1 cup water
¼ cup sugar
¼ cup oil
1 tablespoon salt
1 egg, room temperature
2 tablespoons butter, melted

Soak raisins in rum 1 hour. Stir together 2 cups flour and yeast. Heat together milk, water, sugar, oil, and salt over low heat until very warm to touch (120°F.). Add liquid ingredients to flour mixture and beat until smooth. Blend in egg. Stir in enough additional flour to make a moderately soft dough. Knead on lightly floured surface until smooth and satiny, 8–10 minutes. Cover dough with upside-down bowl and let rest 20 minutes. Divide dough in half. Roll each portion to 7x14-inch rectangle. Brush with melted butter and sprinkle each with half of the raisin-rum mixture. Beginning at narrow side, roll up tightly, pressing dough into roll at each turn. Press ends to seal and fold ends under loaf. Place in two greased 4½x8½-inch loaf pans. Let rise in warm place (80–85°F.) until doubled, about 45 minutes. Bake in preheated 375°F. oven 35–40 minutes. Remove immediately from pans; cool on wire rack.

2 loaves

SUGAR-CRUMB CAKE

- **3 cups flour**
- **1 package dry yeast**
- **¾ cup milk**
- **1 cup butter**
- **¼ cup Mr. Boston Crème de Noyaux**
- **¼ cup sugar**
- **1 teaspoon grated lemon peel**
- **1 teaspoon salt**
- **2 eggs, room temperature**
- **Streusel Topping (see below)**

Stir together 1 cup flour and yeast. Heat together milk, butter, Crème de Noyaux, sugar, lemon peel, and salt until very warm to touch (120°F.). Add to flour mixture and beat until smooth. Add eggs and beat until smooth. Add remaining flour, a cup or so at a time, beating well after each addition. Continue to beat until mixture forms a soft dough. Knead on lightly floured surface until smooth and elastic, about 10 minutes. Place dough in greased bowl, and turn to grease all sides. Cover and let rise in warm place (80–85°F.) until doubled in bulk, about 40 minutes. Punch down. Knead on lightly floured surface 3–4 minutes. Place in greased 15½ x 10½-inch jelly-roll pan; spread out with hands or rolling pin until dough covers bottom of pan. Sprinkle Streusel Topping evenly over cake. Bake in preheated 375°F. oven 40–45 minutes or until the top is crusty. Serve warm or at room temperature.

one 10½x15½-inch cake

Streusel Topping

- **1 cup flour**
- **⅓ cup sugar**
- **½ teaspoon cinnamon**
- **½ cup butter**

Stir together flour, sugar, and cinnamon. Cut butter into dry ingredients until mixture resembles coarse crumbs. Distribute evenly over cake before baking.

AUSTRIAN ALMOND BRAID

- 5–5½ cups flour
- 2 packages dry yeast
- 1 cup milk
- ⅓ cup sugar
- ½ cup butter
- ¼ cup Amaretto di Saronno
- 2 teaspoons salt
- 2 eggs, room temperature
- ½ cup golden raisins
- ½ cup candied mixed fruit, chopped
- ½ cup chopped blanched almonds
- Oil
- Almond icing (see below)
- Candied fruit (optional)
- Chopped nuts (optional)

Stir together 2 cups flour and yeast. Heat together milk, sugar, butter, Amaretto di Saronno, and salt until very warm to touch (120°F.). Add liquid ingredients to flour mixture and beat until smooth. Blend in eggs. Add 1 cup flour and beat 1 minute. Stir in raisins, fruit, and almonds; add more flour to make a soft dough. Knead on lightly floured surface until smooth and satiny, 8–10 minutes. Place dough in greased bowl and turn to grease all sides. Cover and let rise in warm place (80–85°F.) until doubled in bulk, about 1½ hours. Punch down; divide dough in half. For each braid, take two-thirds of each portion of dough and divide into thirds. Roll each third into a 15-inch strand. Form two braids on lightly greased baking sheet. Divide each remaining third into thirds and form six 18-inch strands. Form two loose braids; place one on top of each braid, pressing in lightly. Tuck ends of top braid under ends of bottom braid. Brush with oil and let rise in warm place (80–85°F.) until doubled, about 45 minutes. Bake in preheated 350°F. oven 25–30 minutes, or until golden brown. Remove from baking sheets to cooling rack. Ice braids with Almond Icing while still slightly warm. Decorate with candied fruit and nuts, if desired.

2 loaves

Almond Icing

- 1½ cups confectioners' sugar
- 1 tablespoon milk
- 1 tablespoon Amaretto di Saronno

Blend all ingredients until smooth and spread over warm cake.

RUSSIAN KULICH

Combine raisins, candied fruits, and Crème de Noyaux; let stand 1 hour. Stir together 1 cup flour and yeast. Heat together 1 cup milk, sugar, oil, and salt over low heat until very warm to touch (120°F.). Add liquid ingredients to flour mixture and beat until smooth, about 2 minutes. Beat in eggs, lemon peel, almonds, and marinated raisins and candied fruit. Add 1 cup flour and beat 1 minute. Stir in enough additional flour to make a soft dough. Knead on lightly floured surface until smooth and satiny, 8–10 minutes. Place in lightly greased bowl, turning dough to grease all sides. Cover and let rise in warm place (80–85°F.) until doubled, about 1½ hours. Punch down. Divide dough into two or three equal portions and shape into balls. Let rest 10 minutes. Grease two 46-ounce juice cans or three 16-ounce coffee cans. Place dough in cans, filling each about half full; brush top with oil. Let rise until doubled, about 1 hour. Bake upright in preheated 350°F. oven 30–35 minutes, or until golden brown. Remove from cans immediately and cool. Blend confectioners' sugar and remaining 1 tablespoon milk until smooth; spread mixture on loaves. Decorate tops with additional candied fruit, if desired.

3 medium or 2 large loaves

¼ cup raisins
¼ cup chopped candied citron
¼ cup chopped candied orange peel
¼ cup chopped candied cherries
⅓ cup Mr. Boston Crème de Noyaux
5 cups flour
2 packages dry yeast
1 cup plus 1 tablespoon milk
⅓ cup sugar
¼ cup oil
2 teaspoons salt
2 eggs, room temperature
2 teaspoons grated lemon peel
½ cup chopped blanched almonds
½ cup confectioners' sugar
Additional candied fruit (optional)

PEACHY WHOLE-WHEAT RING

3–3½ cups all-purpose flour
2 packages dry yeast
½ teaspoon nutmeg
¾ cup milk
¼ cup Mr. Boston Peach Flavored Brandy
¼ cup water
¼ cup oil
½ cup honey
2 teaspoons salt
2 eggs, room temperature
2 cups whole wheat flour
2 tablespoons butter, melted
½ cup light brown sugar, packed
½ cup chopped pecans
1 tablespoon cinnamon
Peachy Glaze (see below)

Stir together 2 cups flour, yeast, and nutmeg. Heat together milk, brandy, water, oil, honey, and salt until very warm to touch (120°F.). Add liquid to flour mixture and beat until smooth. Beat in eggs. Blend in 1 cup whole wheat flour; beat 1 minute more. Let rest 5 minutes. Add the remaining whole wheat flour and enough all-purpose flour to make a soft dough. Knead on a lightly floured surface until smooth and satiny, 8–10 minutes. Place dough in greased bowl and turn to grease all sides. Let rise in warm place (80–85°F.) until doubled in bulk, 1–1½ hours. Punch down and let rest 10 minutes. Divide in half. Roll each half into an 8x15-inch rectangle. Brush with melted butter. Stir together brown sugar, nuts, and cinnamon. Sprinkle mixture over dough. Roll up jelly-roll fashion, sealing edges. Form each into a ring on greased baking sheet. Cut almost through ring in slices about 1 inch thick. Turn each slice slightly. Let rise in warm place about 30–45 minutes. Bake in preheated 350°F. oven 25–30 minutes. Frost with Peachy Glaze, if desired.

2 coffeecakes

Peachy Glaze

1½ cups confectioners' sugar
1 tablespoon Mr. Boston Peach Flavored Brandy
3–4 tablespoons milk

Combine sugar, brandy, and enough milk to attain drizzling consistency. Drizzle over warm cake.

HUNGARIAN CHRISTMAS BREAD

Stir together 2 cups flour and yeast. Heat together milk, sugar, water, 1/4 cup rum, oil, and salt until very warm to touch (120°F.). Add liquid ingredients to flour mixture and beat until smooth, about 2 minutes. Blend in 2 eggs. Add 1 cup flour and beat 1 minute. Stir in enough additional flour to make a moderately stiff dough. Knead on lightly floured surface until smooth and satiny, 5–8 minutes. Cover with pan or bowl and let rest 30 minutes. Divide in half. Roll each half into a 10x12-inch rectangle. Combine poppy seed filling and remaining 1 tablespoon rum. Spread filling over dough, leaving 1-inch margin on all sides; sprinkle with raisins. Roll up jelly-roll fashion. Seal bottom and ends securely. Place on greased baking sheet, seam side down. Make shallow, diagonal cuts across top. Beat remaining egg; brush over tops and sides of dough. Sprinkle generously with poppy seeds. Let rise in warm place (80–85°F.) until doubled, about 45 minutes. Bake in preheated 350°F. oven 30–40 minutes.

2 loaves

4½–5 cups flour
2 packages dry yeast
½ cup milk
½ cup sugar
¼ cup water
¼ cup plus 1 tablespoon Mr. Boston Virgin Islands Rum
¼ cup oil
2 teaspoons salt
3 eggs, room temperature
1 twelve-ounce can poppy cake and pastry filling
1 cup golden raisins
Poppy seeds

TIPSY CRULLERS

- ½ cup water
- ½ cup Amaretto di Saronno
- ¼ cup butter
- ¼ teaspoon salt
- 1 cup flour
- 4 eggs
- Oil
- 2 cups sifted confectioners' sugar
- 3 tablespoons Amaretto di Saronno
- Colored sprinkles

Bring water, Amaretto di Saronno, butter, and salt to a boil. Stir in flour all at once and beat until mixture forms a ball. Remove from heat and beat in eggs, one at a time. Place dough in pastry bag fitted with large star tip. Brush pancake turner with oil. Pipe a circle of dough onto turner. Place in 1–1½ inches hot oil and fry for 1 minute. Carefully remove cruller from turner with sharp knife. Turn and fry until golden brown on both sides. Remove from pan, drain, and cool. Repeat, until all dough is used. Combine confectioners' sugar and Amaretto di Saronno. Mix until smooth. Spoon over crullers. Dip crullers in colored sprinkles. Let stand until icing is set. Serve immediately.

14 crullers

Tipsy Crullers

Crepes

ILLVA
AMARETTO
di
SARONNO®
ORIGINALE
A LIQUEUR PRODUCED BY
ILLVA SARONNO ITALY

CARDAMOM BRAID

5½–6 cups flour
2 packages dry yeast
½ cup milk
¼ cup water
¼ cup Mr. Boston Triple Sec
½ cup butter
⅓ cup sugar
1 teaspoon salt
1½ teaspoons ground cardamom
3 eggs, room temperature
1 cup raisins
1 cup candied citron
1 cup slivered almonds

Stir together 2 cups flour and yeast. Heat together milk, water, triple sec, butter, sugar, salt, and cardamom until very warm to touch (120°F.). Add liquid to flour mixture and beat until smooth, about 2 minutes. Add eggs; beat well. Add 1 cup flour and beat 1 minute. Stir in raisins, citron, and half the almonds. Add enough additional flour to make moderately stiff dough. Knead on lightly floured surface until smooth and satiny, 8–10 minutes. Place in greased bowl, turning dough to grease all sides. Let rise in warm place (80–85°F.) until doubled, about 1½ hours. Punch down and let rest 10 minutes. Divide dough in half. Divide each half into 3 equal pieces. Roll each piece into 15-inch strip, 1 inch in diameter. On greased baking sheet, form into two braids, folding ends under. Let rise in warm place until doubled, about 45 minutes. Sprinkle with remaining almonds. Bake in preheated 350°F. oven 35–40 minutes.

2 braids

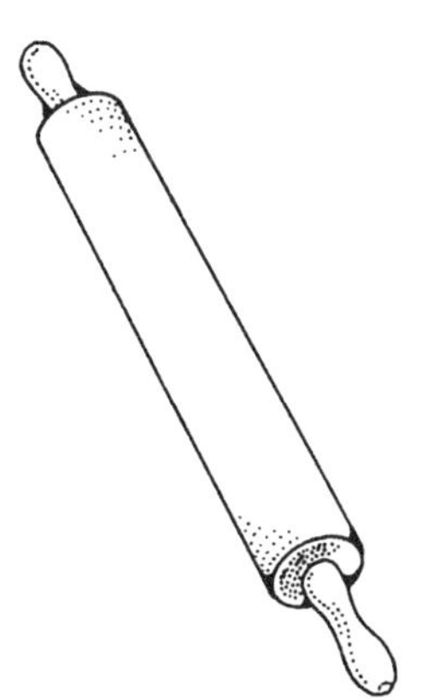

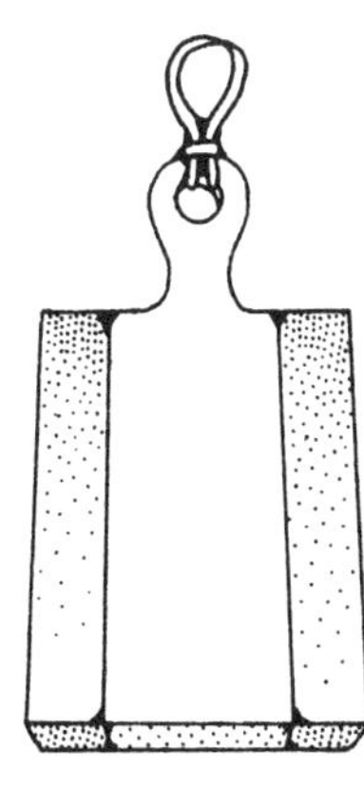

KUGELHUPF

1 cup raisins
⅓ cup Mr. Boston Virgin Islands Dark Rum
3–4 cups flour
2 packages dry yeast
1 cup milk
½ cup water
½ cup sugar
½ cup butter
1 teaspoon salt
3 eggs, room temperature
Butter, softened
⅓ cup ground almonds
Sifted confectioners' sugar
Candied fruits
Nuts
Corn syrup

Soak raisins in rum 10–20 minutes. Stir together 2 cups flour and yeast. Heat together milk, water, sugar, ½ cup butter, and salt until very warm to touch (120°F.). Add warm liquid ingredients to flour mixture and beat until smooth. Blend in eggs; add ½ cup flour and beat 2 minutes. Add enough additional flour to make a thick batter. Cover and let rise in warm place (80–85°F.) until batter is doubled in volume and bubbly, about 1 hour. Stir down. Spoon into two 1½-quart or three 1-quart fancy molds that have been buttered and dusted with ground almonds. Cover and let rise in warm place until doubled, about 30 minutes. Bake in preheated 325°F. oven 1 hour for 1½-quart loaves or 45 minutes for 1-quart loaves. Unmold on wire racks. Dust with confectioners' sugar. Decorate with candied fruits and nuts that have been dipped in corn syrup.

2 large or
3 small loaves

Create Your Own . . .

This book is but a beginning. If you have come to this point, you are prepared to find out what happens in other cases when you add a hint of this liqueur or a dash of that spirit. Begin modestly. Test your handiwork personally and with others. Innovate. Keep records.

We have selected as basics dessert crêpes, Napoleons, cheesecakes, tortes, mousse, and a sauce. We use one spirit in each and list others that you may wish to try. But don't stop there.

A second step might be to change the spirit used in these recipes. Only remember that such changes are more than cosmetic. They affect the chemistry of taste and the interaction of many ingredients.

With the ingredients at hand and the formulas for desserts already presented in this book, you have everything required. You know what happens "when." So find out what happens "if." Ultimately you will create your own original formulas. While success depends on the basic recipe and the kind of spirit you select, it relies even more on your own imagination and good taste.

CREATE-YOUR-OWN DESSERT CRÊPE

1 eight-ounce package cream cheese, softened
1 cup chopped fruit*
2 tablespoons Mr. Boston liqueur*
1 tablespoon sugar
10–12 5-inch crepes
Confectioner's sugar
Slivered almonds

Blend cream cheese, fruit, liqueur, and sugar until smooth. Spread about 2 tablespoons filling down center of each crêpe. Fold crêpe around filling. Sprinkle with confectioners' sugar and almonds. To serve warm, place crepes in 9x13-inch baking pan, cover, and heat in preheated 350°F. oven 15–20 minutes. Sprinkle with confectioners' sugar and almonds. Serve immediately.

5–6 servings

*Use:
Strawberries with Amaretto di Saronno or Mr. Boston Crème de Cacao
Oranges with Mr. Boston Triple Sec or Mandarine Napoleon
Blueberries with Mr. Boston Crème de Cassis
Peaches with Amaretto di Saronno
Bananas with Mr. Boston Crème de Banana
Cherries with Mr. Boston Cherry Flavored Brandy

CREATE-YOUR-OWN NAPOLEON

1 ten-inch square frozen puff pastry, thawed
1 package (4⅛ ounces) instant vanilla pudding
¾ cup sour cream
½ cup milk
¼ cup Mr. Boston liqueur*
2 one-ounce squares semi-sweet chocolate

Roll puff pastry sheet out to 10x16-inch rectangle. Cut into four 4x10-inch rectangles. Place on ungreased baking sheet and prick. Bake in preheated 350°F. oven 20–25 minutes or until golden brown. Blend pudding mix, sour cream, milk, and 2 tablespoons liqueur until smooth; refrigerate until thickened. Stack puff pastry layers, spreading a third of the pudding mixture between each two layers. Melt chocolate with remaining 2 tablespoons liqueur over low heat, stirring constantly, until smooth. Spread over top. Chill until ready to serve.

8–10 servings

*Use:
Amaretto di Saronno
Mr. Boston Triple Sec
Mr. Boston Cherry Flavored Brandy
Mr. Boston Crème de Cacao
Mr. Boston Crème de Menthe
Mr. Boston Anisette

CREATE-YOUR-OWN CHEESECAKE

3 cups coarse graham cracker crumbs
½ cup butter, melted
1 fifteen-ounce carton ricotta cheese
1 eight-ounce package cream cheese
4 eggs, lightly beaten
½ cup sugar
¼ cup Mr. Boston liqueur*
¼ teaspoon salt

Combine crumbs and butter; press over bottom and sides of greased 9-inch springform pan or 10-inch pie pan. Beat together ricotta and cream cheese until smooth. Add eggs, sugar, liqueur, and salt; beat until smooth. Pour mixture into pan. Bake in preheated 325°F. oven 1 hour and 15 minutes or until firm in middle. Cool 20–30 minutes in pan before removing. Cool completely before serving.

one 9-inch cheesecake

*Use:
Mr. Boston Triple Sec
Mr. Boston Crème de Cacao
Mr. Boston Anisette
Amaretto di Saronno
Mr. Boston Crème de Banana
Mr. Boston Coffee Flavored Brandy

FAVORITE FRUIT BRANDY SAUCE

1 sixteen-ounce can fruit, drained; reserve ¾ cup juice*
2 tablespoons cornstarch
½ cup Mr. Boston Flavored Brandy*
½ teaspoon cinnamon

Bring ½ cup juice to boil. Combine remaining juice with cornstarch. Stir cornstarch mixture, brandy, and cinnamon into boiling liquid. Reduce heat and cook, stirring constantly, until mixture is smooth and thickened. Stir in fruit and cook until thoroughly heated. Serve warm sauce over ice cream, pound cake, pudding, or custard.

Makes 2 cups

*Use:
Mr. Boston Peach Flavored Brandy and peaches
Mr. Boston Apricot Flavored Brandy and apricots
Mr. Boston Cherry Flavored Brandy and cherries
Mr. Boston Ginger Flavored Brandy and pears
Mr. Boston Blackberry Flavored Brandy and blackberries

FAVORITE DRINK MOUSSE

- **1 envelope (1 tablespoon) unflavored gelatin**
- **6 tablespoons water**
- **¾ cup of your favorite drink***
- **5 eggs, separated**
- **¾ cup sugar**
- **1 cup heavy cream, whipped**

Sprinkle gelatin over 4 tablespoons water in saucepan; let stand 5 minutes. Heat mixture until gelatin dissolves and mixture comes to a boil. Remove from heat and stir in your favorite drink. Chill until mixture is slightly thickened 15–20 minutes. Beat egg yolks, ½ cup sugar, and remaining 2 tablespoons water until thick and lemon-colored. Beat in chilled gelatin mixture. Beat egg whites until foamy. Gradually add ¼ cup sugar and continue beating until stiff, but not dry, peaks form. Fold yolk mixture into whites. Fold egg mixture into whipped cream. Pour into 6-cup soufflé dish, add collar if necessary, and chill 3–4 hours or until set.

8–10 servings

***Whiskey Sour**
½ cup lemon juice
¼ cup Old Thompson Blended Whiskey

Daiquiri
½ cup lime juice
¼ cup Mr. Boston Virgin Islands Light Rum

Screwdriver
½ cup orange juice
¼ cup Glenmore Vodka

Irish Coffee
½ cup coffee
¼ cup Old Thompson Blended Whiskey

Tom Collins
½ cup lemon juice
¼ cup Glenmore Gin

Black Russian
¼ cup Glenmore Vodka
2 tablespoons Mr. Boston Coffee Flavored Brandy
6 tablespoons water

CREATE-YOUR-OWN TORTE

Slice pound cake lengthwise into 4 layers. Brush each layer with liqueur. Spread each layer with 1–2 tablespoons preserves. Combine half the whipped cream with cocoa; spread half the chocolate mixture over bottom layer; top with next layer. Spread half the plain whipped cream over second layer; top with sliced fruit. Top with next layer. Spread with remaining chocolate mixture. Sprinkle with nuts. Top with remaining layer and spread with remaining plain whipped cream. Refrigerate until serving time.

6–8 servings

*Use:
Amaretto di Saronno with peaches or cherries and pecans
Mr. Boston Crème de Banana with bananas and walnuts or almonds
Mr. Boston Triple Sec with strawberries or mandarin orange sections and pecans or almonds
Mr. Boston Crème de Cacao with strawberries, oranges, or raspberries and almonds
Mr. Boston Crème de Cassis with blueberries or raspberries and pecans or filberts
Mr. Boston Anisette with chopped candied fruit and almonds

10¾–11 ounces pound cake
¼–⅓ cup Mr. Boston liqueur*
⅓–½ cup preserves
1 cup heavy cream, whipped
1½ teaspoons cocoa
½–¾ cup sliced fruit*
¼ cup coarsely chopped nuts

LIQUOR INDEX

BRANDIES

Mr. Boston Five Star Brandy

FLAVORED BRANDIES

Mr. Boston Apricot Flavored Brandy

Mr. Boston Blackberry Flavored Brandy

Mr. Boston Coffee Flavored Brandy

Mr. Boston Ginger Flavored Brandy

Mr. Boston Peach Flavored Brandy

Mr. Boston Cherry Flavored Brandy

Rémy Martin V.S.O.P. Cognac

Strawberry Ice Cream Roll, 33
Strawberry Cream Puff Ring, 81
Chocolate-Cognac Flan with Chocolate Sauce, 17
Festive Kugel, 18
Melon in Cognac, 6

CORDIALS

Mr. Boston Crème de Menthe (green or white)

Crème de Menthe Sherbet, 37
Minted Butter Cookies, 68
Mint Brownie Pie, 79

Mr. Boston Crème de Cacao (brown and white)

Mocha Pound Cake with Creamy Chocolate Glaze, 55
Strawberry Crown Torte with Chocolate Frosting, 60
Cherry-Chocolate Torte, 57
Strawberry Mocha Cassata, 39
Brandy Alexander Tartlets, 83
Mint Brownie Pie, 79
Mocha Mousse, 19
Chocolate-Cognac Flan with Chocolate Sauce, 17
Banana Surprise Cake, 49

Expresso Coffee Liqueur

Mocha Mousse, 19

Mr. Boston Crème de Cassis

Chocolate Raspberry Cake, 52
Yogurt Cake, 47
Cranberry Cassis Pie, 78
Raspberry Soufflé, 16
Plum Coffee Cake, 95

Mr. Boston Peppermint Schnapps

Peppermint Schnapps Parfait, 34
Pink Peppermint Pie, 86

Mr. Boston Anisette

Snowball, 35
Fennel Cakes, 66
Hearty Pear Bread, 89

Mr. Boston Crème de Banana

Banana Surprise Cake, 49
Banana Daiquiri Pie, 77
Banana Cream Pie, 76

Mr. Boston Triple Sec

Orange Blossom Cake, 54
Bolo de Laranga, 48
Soufflé Glacé à la Orange, 30
Pear Sorbet, 34
Orange Chocolate Chip Cookies, 67
Orange Caraway Cookies, 68
Italian Anise Biscotti, 70
Fruit Flan, 82
Marguerita Pie, 79
Creamy Orange Caramel, 18
Orange Nut Swirls, 91
Orange Almond Syrup, 94
Cardamom Braid, 105

Mr. Boston Crème de Noyaux

Easy Peach Almond Cobbler, 8
Sugar-Crumb Cake, 99
Russian Kulich, 101

Mr. Boston Rock & Rye

Glazed Apple Dumplings, 84

Amaretto di Saronno

Strawberry Crown Torte, 60
Mocha Cheesecake Saronno, 44
Chocolate Mousse Cake Saronno, 43
Chocolate Almond Ice Cream, 33

RECIPE INDEX